WHAT IS COUNTERTERRORISM FOR?

The status quo is broken. The world is grappling with a web of challenges that could threaten our very existence. If we believe in a better world, now is the time to question the purpose behind our actions and those taken in our name.

Enter the What Is It For? series – a bold exploration of the core elements shaping our world, from religion and free speech to animal rights and the war. This series cuts through the noise to reveal the true impact of these topics, what they really do and why they matter.

Ditching the usual heated debates and polarisations, this series offers fresh, forward-thinking insights. Leading experts present groundbreaking ideas and point to ways forward for real change, urging us to envision a brighter future.

Each book dives into the history and function of its subject, uncovering its role in society and, crucially, how it can be better.

Series editor: George Miller

Visit **bristoluniversitypress.co.uk/what-is-it-for** to find out more about the series.

LEONIE B. JACKSON is Assistant Professor of International Relations at Northumbria University. She is the author of several articles and books on the representation of terrorism and counterterrorism and serves as an editor of the journal *Critical Studies on Terrorism*.

WHAT IS COUNTERTERRORISM FOR?

LEONIE B. JACKSON

First published in Great Britain in 2025 by

Bristol University Press
University of Bristol
1–9 Old Park Hill
Bristol
BS2 8BB
UK
t: +44 (0)117 374 6645
e: bup-info@bristol.ac.uk

Details of international sales and distribution partners are available at
bristoluniversitypress.co.uk

© Leonie B. Jackson 2025

British Library Cataloguing in Publication Data
A catalogue record for this book is available from the British Library

ISBN 978-1-5292-3459-6 paperback
ISBN 978-1-5292-3460-2 ePub
ISBN 978-1-5292-3461-9 ePdf

Dedicated to Sian, who is always
a bright light in the darkness

CONTENTS

LIST OF FIGURES

ACKNOWLEDGEMENTS

I am immensely grateful to the community of students and colleagues with whom I have discussed terrorism and counterterrorism over the years and who have helped shaped this book. Particular thanks go to George Kassimeris, Catherine McGlynn, Shaun McDaid, Kirsten Haack, Helena Farrand Carrapico and Louisa Rogers. Thanks also to George Miller at Bristol University Press, whose careful editing has improved the project at every step.

I am especially (and forever) indebted to Ariane Bogain, whose comments on an early draft have been invaluable, and whose company always manages to make the graft of scholarship a pleasure. Any remaining errors are, of course, my own.

Finally, thanks as ever to Simon Hayward who has joined me enthusiastically in every adventure and supported me with grace and empathy through all the ups and downs of writing this book, and with life in general.

1
WHAT IS COUNTERTERRORISM?

In the 21st century counterterrorism has become a part of our everyday lives and we are constantly told that terrorism is one of the biggest threats to our own security and to international stability. To counter this, states have engaged in spectacular and enduring wars, extensive changes to legal frameworks, and security operations that include the targeted killing and preventive detention of suspected militants. Through these campaigns, the everyday lives of billions of people have changed in both violent and banal ways. Those within countries targeted by counterterrorism forces have found themselves subjected to extraordinary levels of violence in both active war zones and territories where undeclared wars rain missiles on suspects and the unlucky civilians who happen to be near. Outside these zones, citizens are asked to watch for and report on potential radicals, while extensive surveillance technology monitors public space and private activities. That there have been extensive and costly efforts to counter terrorism this century is beyond doubt, but what has all this frenetic activity actually been *for*?

While terrorism is a tactic that can be used from above or below (that is, by the state or by non-state groups), counterterrorism is exclusively a state phenomenon and consists of the practices and approaches used by various arms of government and security services to prevent and disrupt challenger groups who use (or are said to use) terrorism. These in turn rely on an understanding of what terrorism is at any given historical moment and the threat that it poses to the targeted state and the people within. Terrorism is famously difficult to characterize, but most definitions consider it a communicative strategy where the threat or use of violence against non-combatants is employed to send a message to a wider audience for a political purpose.[1]

Although the state is almost as difficult to define as terrorism, one of the earliest and most concise attempts to characterize it comes from German sociologist Max Weber, who argued:

> [A] state is a human community that (successfully) claims the monopoly of the legitimate use of physical force within a given territory ... the right to use physical force is ascribed to other institutions or to individuals only to the extent to which the state permits it. The state is considered the sole source of the 'right' to use violence.[2]

Modern states are built on the requirement that those within their territories surrender the natural right to use violence against others in exchange for the state's protection against internal and external threats. This is, in essence, the foundation of the social contract. Thomas Hobbes, writing during the English Civil War, famously argued that surrendering liberty to the sovereign was preferable to life in a state of nature that was 'nasty, brutish and short', and the extent of personal liberty to be relinquished in return for security was central to the debates of Enlightenment thinkers in the 18th century and their revolutionary projects in America and France. As we shall see, the relative priority given to liberty versus security remains fundamental to understanding counterterrorism today.

Since the state claims the sole right to employ violence, the use of terrorism by non-state groups is particularly problematic because, through violence or its threat, terrorism spectacularly communicates that the state has lost control of its founding claim at the same time as demonstrating that it cannot protect those within its territory. Counterterrorism is the state's response to this and is itself a communicative strategy that seeks to reassure citizens and repair the social contract by showing that something *is* being done, while simultaneously reasserting its right to the monopoly on violence. The danger in the design and implementation of these measures, however, is that the cure may be worse than the disease.

The argument of this book is that counterterrorism in the 21st century has itself eroded the social contract, creating long-lasting and profound changes to the ways states and citizens relate. Extensive coercive powers have been claimed to watch, target, detain and punish individuals suspected of terrorism. And while these have usually started out as exceptional practices and emergency legislation, such powers are rarely surrendered voluntarily, and they frequently expand well beyond their original function. What begins as a state of exception aimed at a narrow group of people increasingly becomes the normal way of doing things, extended to a broader population and used for purposes other than countering terrorism. We find ourselves, in the third decade of this century, in a situation where national and global norms (including state sovereignty, human rights, civil liberties and the rule of law) have been, and are still being, eroded through new counterterrorism powers such as the assassination of suspected terrorists, indefinite detention and torture, and changes to due process. And beyond the liberal democratic order, authoritarian states have embraced counterterrorism discourse and practice as a means of ridding themselves of dissidents and troublesome minorities. These practices clearly serve a broader purpose than simply protecting people from terrorism; they allow the state to demonstrate its relevance and necessity. Across the world governments have used extraordinary counterterrorism measures to shore up and expand state power at the expense of citizens.

The key claim that has fuelled the counterterrorism industry in the 21st century is that the attacks against the World Trade Center and Pentagon on 11 September

2001 (9/11) ushered in a new world where the old ways of doing things were no longer suitable. This idea was central to the George W. Bush administration's preventive approach to counterterrorism via the war on terror, and its demand that the world choose sides: 'Every nation, in every region, now has a decision to make. Either you are with us, or you are with the terrorists.'[3] These claims, that the world changed on 9/11 and that the battle lines had been drawn, have together generated a truly extraordinary expansion of counterterrorism across the world (see Chapter 2).

Figure 1.1: The aftermath of two airplanes crashing into the World Trade Center, New York, on 11 September 2001

Yet while *perceptions* of terrorism (particularly for the American public and media) certainly did change after 2001, transnational terrorist attacks themselves actually changed very little. Those groups, tactics and targets that existed before 9/11 continued to exist after this event, and the chances of being a victim of terrorism, especially outside of conflict zones and in the global North, remain very small. The annual fatality risk from terrorism in Western Europe, for example, is around one in 3.5 million.[4] This begs the question as to why terrorism, which causes relatively few casualties, generates such great anxiety that people are willing to support huge transfers of money and personnel to the counterterrorism sector, along with costly wars and profound changes to their daily lives. These approaches are possible because of the way terrorism is framed, and the key to understanding what counterterrorism is *for* lies in understanding how the thing it is supposed to be countering – terrorism – is represented.

Framing terrorism

How we talk about terrorism matters. This is reflected in the old cliché that one person's terrorist is another's freedom fighter, and it points to an important problem when studying terrorism and counterterrorism: the way we understand an issue has enormous implications for the way we deal with it.

Responding to terrorism is made more complex by the famous inability to agree on what it actually is. Academics and experts disagree on precisely what they are analysing, with one study cataloguing 109 different scholarly definitions.[5] There is similarly little consensus among states, and most do not include state terrorism in their definitions, concentrating instead on non-state groups' use of terrorism rather than state use of terrorist tactics against their own populations (although state-*sponsored* terrorism, that is, that which emerges from 'rogue' states against other states, is sometimes included). Even within states different agencies have different understandings of the phenomenon. For example, the US's Federal Bureau of Investigation defines international terrorism as 'violent, criminal acts committed by individuals and/or groups who are inspired by, or associated with, designated foreign terrorist organizations or nations',[6] while the State Department defines it as 'premeditated, politically motivated violence perpetrated against non-combatant targets by subnational groups or clandestine agents'.[7] One study noted that at least 19 different definitions of terrorism could be found in US federal law.[8]

Understanding a violent act as a crime implies a different set of responsive strategies than if it is represented as an act of war. In the former case we expect the police and criminal justice system to deal with it, while in the latter we expect military and diplomatic actors to take responsibility. The framing of the issue also indicates the magnitude of the problem. There exists within society a set of institutions for dealing with crime, including a specific set of actors (police, judiciary), rules (laws, due process) and consequences (sentences, prison time). All of these function to deal with crime as a social ill, and labelling an act as a crime indicates that it can be dealt with through these institutions. Wars, by contrast, are understood to be more profoundly dangerous to a society. Although wars can be both limited and unlimited in terms of tactics, strategy and goals, the language of war usually seeks to mobilize patriotic fervour and the resources of a society by portraying the enemy as a threat to the continuation and even the existence of a national community or a way of life. While fighting crime often involves the channelling of extensive economic and human resources, fighting a war requires significant changes to everyday life.

The language of war has reappeared frequently in the history of counterterrorism. Following the 1901 shooting of President William McKinley by Polish-American anarchist Leon Czolgosz, Vice-President Theodore Roosevelt argued that 'we should war with relentless efficiency not only against anarchists, but against all active and passive sympathizers with anarchists'.[9] During a wave of leftist terrorism in the 1970s, Uruguayan foreign minister Juan Carlos Blanco Estradé claimed the violence amounted to a 'Third World War' that justified Operation Condor, the torture and murder of 'subversives' by the South American military dictatorships, who regarded themselves as the last bastion of Christian civilization.[10] And President Ronald Reagan used the language of war to depict Libyan-sponsored terrorism and the US response in his 1985 declaration that 'under international law, any state which is the victim of acts of war has the right to defend itself'.[11] Yet, even when not openly described as a war, the amorphous and slippery nature of terrorism has historically proven useful for political elites, who can point to the threat posed by challenger groups to justify bolstering their own power through the declaration of emergency measures and the suspension of constitutional protections and the rule of law. As I shall discuss in Chapter 3, terrorism has frequently been presented as the fundamental danger within the global system, threatening to tip the world into anarchy and requiring robust counterterrorist measures to protect a besieged civilization.

Figure 1.2: Assassination of President McKinley at Pan-American Exposition reception, 6 September 1901

Photograph of wash drawing by T. Dart Walker, c. 1905.

The language of good and evil has also made frequent reappearances in talk of terrorism, placing particular groups and individuals outside of human rationality. Since evil cannot be negotiated with (only defeated), all rules may be justifiably suspended in countering terrorism if it is viewed as a manifestation of evil. And both states and the groups challenging them draw on this construct in their justifications for action: George W. Bush's characterization of the 9/11 hijackers as 'evildoers' directly mirrored Osama bin Laden's account of the US army as 'the soldiers of Satan'. Within this representational world, political elites, challenger groups, victims, the media, experts and the public all present their own preferred account when talking about terrorism. Counterterrorism is very much part of this process and is itself a story over which differently situated actors wrestle to control the narrative.

Securitization

Securitization is a specific type of framing that moves an issue into the realm of security and therefore demands special powers to deal with it. As a form of storytelling, securitization presents a narrative about an existential threat, identifying who or what is endangered (often by assigning heroic/villainous identities), warning what could happen if the threat is ignored, and identifying a way out of this predicament if certain rules or ways of doing things are altered. Securitization requires several steps:[12]

- identification of a threat to a collective (usually states or nations, but can be other groups);
- a securitizing actor (who declares that the threat is existential);

- an audience (to whom the story is directed and who must be convinced that the security measures proposed are necessary and that rules must be broken).

Once a security situation is accepted, the usual rules of the game may be suspended, and new powers can be claimed to focus society's energies on the task of dealing with the security threat. But audiences must accept the security stories told in order for these changes to happen; not all securitizations will be accepted.

This is why framing is so important. By tapping into sociocultural beliefs about specific threats, audiences will be more likely to accept securitizations, and because of this a familiar set of stories is often repeated in times of crisis. For example, the understanding that the 1938 Munich agreement represented the appeasement of Hitler has been drawn on time and again to securitize situations and justify extraordinary powers. By appealing to socially shared understandings of the Second World War as a 'good' war against 'evil', and the Munich agreement as the wrong-headed appeasement of Nazi expansionism, other threats have been securitized by comparing them to 1938. These include President Truman's characterization of the North Korean attack against the South in 1950, President Kennedy's likening of Soviet behaviour in the Cuban Missile Crisis to Hitler's aggression and Prime Minister Blair's characterization of events in Kosovo (1999).[13] By framing contemporary events as analogous to the appeasement of Nazi Germany, all these leaders were able to draw on powerful national and global narratives to convince audiences of the need to suspend the norms against military intervention in sovereign states.

While most securitizations happen at national or state level, some – macrosecuritizations – happen on an international level. These have an umbrella-like function, structuring international security by allowing actors on lower levels to fit their own security concerns into a broader, overarching security story.[14] The Cold War is a good example of this, where many diverse internal and external conflicts were represented under the broad umbrella of the battle between capitalism and communism. This allowed US-aligned states to present their specific struggles against insurgents and rebels as existential because they were framed as part of a larger conflict to protect Western civilization against the perils of international communism, while USSR-aligned states could present themselves as an anti-imperialist coalition that sought to free the oppressed from the chains of global capitalism and Western domination. By drawing on this macrosecuritization a range of benefits were available, including increased financial and military support from superpower sponsors, greater internal and external tolerance for the suspensions of human rights and civil liberties, and ideological identity-related benefits accorded to those who were associated with the 'free world' or 'anti-imperialism'.

The war on terror can be understood as a similar macrosecuritization, which enabled smaller local and regional conflicts with Islamist groups to be represented as part of a global contest of civilization against barbarism and good against evil. Several states took the opportunity after 2001 to represent their local conflicts with insurgent groups as part of the war on terror. President Putin's characterization of the 9/11 attacks as a 'global Chechnya', for example, enabled Russia's Second Chechen War (1999–2009) to be reframed as part of the war on terror, underplaying the separatist struggle that underpinned it and recasting it as part of a global clash of civilizations with Islamist militants. China similarly portrayed the Xinjiang region as a key focus of Osama bin Laden's plans and recast its conflict with Uyghur separatists in the region as a 'People's War on Terror'. By identifying themselves with the 'civilized' and 'good' in this global narrative, states have exploited the macrosecuritization of the war on terror to subsume regional conflicts and to justify the human rights and civil liberty abuses perpetrated in its name.

This book argues that counterterrorism's purpose goes beyond preventing or mitigating terrorist attacks – it is centrally about reasserting and performing state power in the face of terrorism's attack on the social contract. And as each subsequent terrorist attack further undermines the state's claims to be able to protect its citizens, additional securitizations are put forward which demand greater powers to suspend rules. Extraordinary powers to counter terrorism have been readily claimed by states in the 21st century and, through these, states performatively demonstrate that they are doing something about terrorism. But whether these powers actually help to protect civilians and their way of life is far from clear. They have arguably been counterproductive: increasing grievances and creating spirals of violence that have rendered people across the world less secure, as well as undermining norms both within states and within international society. The sheer economic, military and coercive power of states means that the waging of counterterrorism potentially represents a far greater existential threat to contemporary ways of life than terrorism itself.

While the present way of countering terrorism is deeply problematic, this book is ultimately optimistic. It argues that there are ways out of the current dilemmas in which we find ourselves. Extensive counterterrorism powers rely on the securitization of terrorism as an existential threat to our way of life, but terrorism can be reframed and desecuritized. It can be taken out of the realm of exceptional practices and placed back into the realm of normal politics. By realistically assessing the risk that terrorism poses, more proportional responses may be devised that respect the rule of law and global human rights norms, and that seek to limit the cycles of violence to which counterterrorism has so often contributed. This book urges us all to reflect, as citizens, on our relationship with the state and the costs we are willing to bear to be protected from terrorism.

2
COUNTERTERRORISM IN
THE 21ST CENTURY

The post-9/11 macrosecuritization of terrorism has relied on the claim that it is a central, and perhaps the most dangerous, threat to all states and peoples in the world today. This has encouraged the development of new ways to counter it that suspend the normal rules of the game, both inside states and in the international arena. But what exactly are the elements of this new approach?

Ronald Crelinsten has divided counterterrorism into two overarching approaches, the criminal justice model and the war model.[1] While each model privileges a particular approach, they are not mutually exclusive: even if the criminal justice model is favoured, military responses are available. And similarly, if a military approach is preferred, legal instruments remain in place and often work alongside. Importantly, both approaches are governed by rules: criminal justice law and the laws of war. However, Crelinsten has argued that in the 21st century a hybrid of these forms has become dominant, which suspends the rules governing each through the discourse and practices of the war on terror. By considering the differences between the criminal justice and war models we can draw out the conceptualizations of terrorism that underpin them as well as the benefits and drawbacks of each in order to understand what, if anything, is 'new' about the hybrid model.

Criminal justice model

The criminal justice model regards terrorism as a crime and draws on the legal system to prevent and respond to terrorist acts, privileging investigative work, the criminal justice system and international cooperation. Following UN Security Council Resolution 1373, adopted on 28 September 2001, almost every state has a law against terrorism and can use its criminal justice system to deter and prosecute terrorist acts. Some states, such as the UK, France and Israel, have had such laws in temporary or permanent form on the books for years, and these are claimed to have both incapacitation and deterrence effects: incapacitating those convicted by removing them to prisons (so they cannot carry out further violent acts) and deterring others who see the consequences of carrying out such crimes and are dissuaded from doing so. Proponents of the criminal justice model argue that it serves rehabilitation purposes, enabling incarcerated offenders to be de-radicalized through the intervention of social workers, counsellors, religious advisors and education professionals to reintegrate them into mainstream society. This approach also has retributive effects, as those convicted are seen by society to get what they deserve, potentially providing some redress for victims of terrorism, who can see that justice is being done.

This approach has two key benefits. First, by treating it as an ordinary crime it de-glorifies and delegitimizes one of the key contentions of those employing terrorism: that they are using violence for a higher purpose. By treating terrorism in the same way as any other criminal act, claims that they are soldiers or freedom fighters are undermined. Second, by using existing criminal justice infrastructure, this approach can deter and punish acts of terrorism through ordinary law enforcement techniques. By using these, counterterrorism can occupy the moral high ground, allowing states to position themselves as ethical vis-à-vis challenger groups, offering the possibility of winning over the constituencies on whose behalf these groups claim to act. This is important because historically one of the strategic aims of terrorism has been to provoke the state into overreaction in order to demonstrate to potential supporters its illegitimacy, hypocrisy and brutality. Established legal processes and checks and balances help to guard against this overreaction, allowing the state to show that it can protect citizens' rights to liberty, security and due process.[2] Further, by treating terrorism as an ongoing problem to be dealt with through the ordinary workings of the criminal justice system, rather than a threat to be eradicated, the issue is framed as manageable.

This model has also been effective. The case of Italy's Red Brigades (*Brigate Rosse*), a far-left group active between 1970 and 1988, is often cited as an example of how the criminal justice system can end a terrorist campaign. By offering plea deals for incarcerated militants in return for intelligence, Italian police were able to use the information gained to dismantle the organization at the same time as providing ways out for those who wanted to leave the group via the Repentance Laws.[3] By raising the cost of remaining in the group and lowering the cost of defection, the Red Brigades' campaign was wound down through ordinary police work and criminal justice measures. Such techniques were also used in the case of the British 'shoe bomber' Richard Reid, who was subdued by crew and passengers while trying to light explosives stashed in his shoes on a December 2001 flight from Paris to Miami. Having been arrested on landing, he was convicted in January 2003, resulting in three consecutive life sentences. But the law enforcement approach employed in this case also facilitated the conviction of a number of others for terrorism offences. Forensic evidence retrieved from Reid's shoes led to the arrest of a co-conspirator, Saajid Badat, who had withdrawn from the operation at the last moment. Badat was convicted in 2005 and received a reduced sentence in return for cooperating with British and US authorities. His testimony was subsequently used in the investigation of other attempted attacks and the prosecution of several high-profile terrorism cases, including those against Adis Medunjanin (who planned to bomb the New York subway system in September 2009), Sulaiman Abu Ghaith (Osama bin Laden's son-in-law, who was extradited from Kuwait to the US and sentenced there to life in prison in September 2014) and Abu Hamza (the former Finsbury Park mosque preacher, who was extradited from the UK to the US and sentenced to life imprisonment in January 2015).

One of the main problems with this model centres on the prosecution of offences and the level of evidence needed to successfully secure a conviction for terrorism. Criminal justice approaches can only prosecute crimes that are on the statute books and terrorism is a tactic that consistently evolves, requiring new laws to keep up with new forms of attack.[4] The lack of laws against skyjacking in the 1970s, for example, meant that effective prosecution of members of the Popular Front for the Liberation of Palestine and other groups using this tactic was difficult until the law caught up. The level of evidence required to secure a conviction can also put prosecutors on the back foot. Given the clandestine nature of groups, large resources are often required for monitoring suspects and gathering proof. Since evidence from one case may impact on both national security (requiring secret evidence and closed-door court proceedings) and on the surveillance and monitoring of other individuals potentially linked to any given group or plot, the decision to prosecute or continue surveillance can be difficult. Also, the presumption of innocence and the burden upon the state to prove guilt beyond reasonable doubt contribute to other potential weaknesses when dealing with terrorism through the criminal justice system. The high standards put in place to prevent innocent people being wrongly convicted mean that there is a strong possibility that dangerous people may be permitted to go free. Given the scale of possible future harm from terrorism, the consequences of this may be particularly grave.

War model

The war model frames terrorism as an act of war or insurgency and prioritizes military responses, particularly the use of force. Armed responses have always been part of the counterterrorism toolbox. Operation Condor as the military response to the 'Third World War' of terrorism has been noted already, but democracies have also been willing to resort to military force in response to terrorist attacks. For example, Canada invoked the War Measures Act to guard MPs in Ottawa after the 1970 kidnapping of a Canadian minister and a British diplomat by the Front de libération du Québec, and Israel launched Operation Peace for Galilee in response to Palestinian Liberation Organization attacks from southern Lebanon in 1982, invading and occupying the country.

The attraction of the war model lies in the speed with which states can respond to attacks, and the clear signal sent to domestic constituencies that something is being done. Since military responses can be carried out unilaterally, action can be swift and decisive, and since they are increasingly underpinned by surveillance and drone technology, action may be less costly to the state in terms of deployment of human resources and international reputation. Israeli targeted killing of suspected terrorists, for example, has often happened without the knowledge of the governments in whose territory these teams operated. Such approaches may have a deterrent effect as well, signalling a state's resolve and illustrating that it will not be intimidated, at the same time as forcing terrorist groups into hiding and making 'safe havens' less secure.

One key problem with the war model is that it confers legitimacy on challenger groups' claims that they are soldiers or freedom fighters. If one of the aims of terrorism is to provoke a state into repressive action in order to evoke sympathy for the group's cause, then the war model approach makes this much more likely. Military responses to terrorism have had a tendency to spill over and escalate violence. The Sri Lankan government's armed response to separatist group the Liberation Tigers of Tamil Eelam (the Tamil Tigers) is a good example of how military measures can hugely intensify violence, in this case leading to a decades-long civil war lasting from the 1980s to 2009. The Indian government's military strike on Amritsar's Golden Temple in 1984, which aimed to clear it of separatist Sikh militants, resulted in the revenge assassination of prime minister Indira Gandhi by her bodyguards a few months later. The anti-Sikh pogroms that followed Gandhi's assassination led to the murder of more than

2,700 Sikhs in Delhi alone, and perhaps thousands more nationwide over six days of rioting.[5]

Other problems of the war model relate closely to its purported benefits. The speed of response and ability to act unilaterally (without UN backing) mean that this approach is reliant on good intelligence, but lack of this can provoke unintended consequences. The 1973 murder of a waiter, Ahmed Bouchikhi, in Norway, by Israeli agents who mistook him for Black September's chief of operations was not only an intelligence disaster, but also revealed the activities of the Israeli Institute for Intelligence and Special Operations (Mossad) on European soil and undermined warm relations between Norway and Israel. The effectiveness of the war model is questionable if not used with care, and military methods may encourage harsh repression against swathes of society, purportedly justified by the need to counter terrorism and protect state security. For example, General Franco attempted in the 1960s and 1970s to crush Euskadi Ta Askatasuna (ETA – Basque Homeland and Freedom) with indiscriminate repression and military force under the 1943 Decree-Law for Repression of Banditry and Terrorism (which was expanded in the 1960s). Targeting particularly the non-violent arms of the broader Basque nationalist movement, the military approach contributed to increased public sympathy for ETA and the loss of state legitimacy in the Basque Country. Nigeria's military response to Islamist militant group Boko Haram in the mid-2000s was marked by collective punishment of those believed to harbour sympathies for the group, including house burning and dragnet arrests, as well as extrajudicial killing of suspected militants and sympathizers.[6] Egypt has similarly used collective punishment, including arbitrary arrests, disappearances, curfews and house demolitions, in its counterterrorism operations against Islamist militants in North Sinai since 2011.[7]

The extent to which the war model of counterterrorism deters (rather than punishes) terrorist attacks is also unclear. While war or the threat of war between states arguably has a deterrent effect, groups employing terrorism may have little interest in the survival of the state in which they operate. And when military retaliation against terrorism is certain, a group will have little incentive to respond to a deterrent threat and alter its behaviour.[8] So, while the war model may have psychological benefits in reasserting state power and demonstrating that something is being done, its function often appears more retaliatory than deterrent.

Both the criminal justice and war models are ideal types, rarely applied in their 'pure' forms. Nevertheless, they both have strengths and weaknesses in specific situations. Importantly, both are governed by legal frameworks that accord rights to those accused (in the criminal justice model) or captured (in the war model). Counterterrorism in the 21st century has increasingly blurred these models, treating terrorism as a special kind of violence, with which ordinary legal codes cannot cope and which must be dealt with via force outside the usual rules of war. The practices associated with the war on terror demonstrate this hybridity, where the rights accorded to those accused or suspected of terrorism have been eroded and the maximal use of force against individuals and groups designated terrorist has become routine.

Hybrid model

Several observers have argued that the 9/11 attacks changed the US's calculations in terms of how to counter terrorism, creating a hybrid model that resulted in abandonment of the legal frameworks that govern both criminal justice and war model responses. Ronald Crelinsten terms this 'September 12th thinking', an approach that emphasizes unilateral and preventive military action and the privileging and legitimization of the use of force through changing (if necessary) the legal rules of the game.[9] The macrosecuritization of terrorism after 2001 as an existential threat to the civilized world has enabled states across the globe to demand new powers to counter it. As a result, norms of behaviour in the domestic and international spheres have been transformed as a new toolbox of approaches to counterterrorism has been created. Three key changes underpin the hybrid model:

- relaxation of the rules on the use of force in the international arena;
- undermining of the laws of war;
- erosion of the domestic rule of law, due process and civil liberties.

The use of force in the international arena (*jus ad bellum*)

Jus ad bellum refers to the Just War principle that governs the conditions under which states can resort to the use of armed force. In the international arena this is governed by the UN Charter, which protects the sovereignty of states by laying down rules for when violent intervention is permitted. The Charter requires members to refrain from the use or threat of force against another state (Article 2(4)), provides for the use of UN authorized violence to maintain or restore international peace and security (Article 42), and allows for states to engage in individual or collective self-defence should they be subjected to an armed attack (Article 51).[10]

Whether pre-emptive force is permitted under the UN Charter was the topic of extensive debates even before 2001, with some maintaining that the use of force prior to an armed attack was not permitted, while others argued for a more liberal interpretation that would allow a state to respond with military force if an attack was imminent. The immediacy of a threat is key here, and the need to demonstrate this derives from an 1837 incident in which the *Caroline*, a US-owned steamship used to aid Canadian rebels against British rule, was set alight and sent over Niagara Falls by an Anglo-Canadian force. In justifying this incident, the British invoked the right of self-defence, to which US Secretary of State, Daniel Webster, replied that self-defence was only legitimate if its necessity was 'instant, overwhelming, leaving no choice of means, and no moment of deliberation' and did nothing unreasonable or excessive.[11] These arguments instituted three specific conditions for pre-emptive action: the imminence of an attack, the necessity of force to prevent it and the proportionality of the response to it. These have since become part of customary international law and were reaffirmed at the Nuremberg Trials when the *Caroline* incident was used to reject arguments that the German invasion of Norway in April 1940 had constituted an act of self-defence (to prevent Britain and France using the country as a base for military operations).

Figure 2.1: Destruction of the American steamboat *Caroline* in December 1837

The 9/11 attacks paved the way for the US to move to unilateral action (without UN backing) and preventive war to counter terrorism. President Bush made it clear that the administration considered the 9/11 attacks an act of war and that the US would respond through military action to states harbouring groups designated as terrorist. The Authorization for the Use of Military Force was passed by Congress on 18 September 2001, granting the president authority to use all necessary force against those who planned, aided or harboured those responsible for the 9/11 attacks. This remains in place today and provides the US with legislative cover to use military force against designated terrorists, while the National Security Strategy 2002, known as the Bush Doctrine, specifically laid out the case for preventive action. Arguing that the US remained under a high level of threat, the Bush Doctrine claimed the right to take 'anticipatory action to defend ourselves, even if uncertainty remains as to the time and place of the enemy's attack. To forestall or prevent such hostile acts by our adversaries, the United States will, if necessary, act pre-emptively'.[12]

Preventive war differs from pre-emptive war in that it seeks to remove a potential threat before it has emerged. While the latter may be acceptable under international norms (if the imminence, necessity and proportionality conditions are met), the former is not. Yet the US administration during the early years of the war on terror constantly (and perhaps deliberately) blurred these two. Sometimes officials talked about pre-emption, for example, when Bush told West Point graduates to be ready to take pre-emptive action, and at other times spoke about prevention, as when Vice President Dick Cheney argued that the invasion of Iraq was necessary to prevent Saddam Hussein getting access to weapons of mass destruction.[13] The US is not the only state to employ these arguments. Israel, for example, has long claimed prevention as legitimate self-defence, using this argument to justify its 1981 bombing of the Osirak nuclear reactor near Baghdad (for which it was condemned by the US and the UN Security Council for violating the norms of international conduct set out in the Charter). However, the US's military might and its insistence on its right to take unilateral preventive action has widened considerably the conditions for preventive war, implanting new international norms that are potentially harmful to the stability of the international order.

The increased use of targeted killing as a counterterrorism measure is important to note here. Since the foundation of the modern state system in Europe, international norms have developed against the use of political assassination as an instrument of foreign policy. During the Renaissance, the assassination of rival heads of state by European leaders was a regular occurrence, however by the 17th century anxieties over the instability generated (along with fears of expected retaliation) instituted a set of norms against the practice. These were codified in the 19th century, in the US through General Order 100 of the 1863 Lieber Code (banning assassination in the context of the Civil War), and in the Declaration of the 1874 Brussels Conference, convened after the Franco-Prussian War. These fed into the First (1899) and Second (1907) Hague Peace Conferences, which prohibited the killing or wounding 'treacherously' of individuals belonging to a hostile nation or army.[14]

The distinction between assassination and targeted killing is muddy and has tended to rest on the idea that assassinations are directed at political figures while targeted killings aim to take out military personnel. In the case of those labelled terrorists, of course, this becomes even more complex, relying on a status that is usually conferred by the very state seeking to remove the individual in question. Defenders of targeted killing as a counterterrorism tool argue that it is a legitimate act of war that may be performed as part of a state's right to self-defence, while critics have argued that it is a form of extrajudicial execution that effectively amounts to assassination.[15]

Initially part of the war on terror in Afghanistan and Iraq, the use of armed drones to target suspected terrorists grew considerably under the Obama administration, moving to theatres outside of conflict zones, such as the Federally Administered Tribal Areas of Pakistan, Yemen and Somalia. This expansion demonstrates the ways that opaque legal justifications for counterterrorism powers can lead to mission creep. Other states have also employed targeted killing to dispose of alleged terrorists. Israel has a long history of targeted killing in its counterterrorism policy, Russia has targeted Chechen militant leaders extensively to counter the insurgency, and Nigeria has been accused of disposing of more than one thousand Boko Haram suspects and sympathizers in this way.[16]

Proponents of targeted killing argue that it meets just war conditions of necessity, by using force only against imminent threats, and proportionality, by reducing the 'collateral damage' of civilian casualties through precision strikes. Further, by taking out terrorists from afar, there is less need to put boots on the ground, reducing the dangers of extensive military operations and the accompanying loss of life.[17] The use of targeted killing thus arguably has benefits over armed conflict; however, it also has a number of intrinsic weaknesses, including the need for excellent intelligence, the tendency for strikes to hit civilians, and the possibility that drone technology may fall into the hands of 'bad actors'. These are explored in more detail in Chapter 4, but for now it is enough to note that hybrid counterterrorism has brought about a situation where norms that guarded against the preventive use of military force have been significantly eroded in the 21st century.

Undermining of international humanitarian law (*jus in bello*)

As *jus ad bellum* governs the conditions under which armed force is acceptable in the international arena, *jus in bello* concerns the rules of conduct when armed conflict is under way. These are embedded in a set of international humanitarian laws that provide minimal protections for actors engaged in war. The hybrid model of counterterrorism has contributed to significant erosion of these established rules through the creation of a new category of actor, 'enemy combatants', who have been detained indefinitely without trial or charge, and the suspension of norms against torture through the 'enhanced interrogation' of those in custody.

Rules of peacetime and wartime determine which laws should apply in the fight against global terrorism, and therefore how those suspected of terrorism should be treated. If terrorism is considered a crime, then law-enforcement rules should apply, which means that detained suspects must be charged and tried. If terrorism is considered war, then those captured on the battlefield may be held as prisoners of war without charge or trial until the end of the conflict. The hybrid approach has blended these rules, and new approaches have developed outside of conventional ways of dealing with suspects, leaving them in legally murky territory where neither the rules of peacetime nor war appear to apply. The key issue here is that the development of hybrid counterterrorism has been intimately tied up with the war on terror, which has neither territorial nor temporal limits. As President Bush stated on 20 September 2001: 'Our war on terror begins with al Qaeda, but it does not end there. It will not end until every terrorist group of global reach has been found, stopped and defeated.'[18] This declaration gave counterterrorist forces an extremely broad range of action. Since the 'war' was against 'terrorists' everywhere, the geographical extent of operations and the individuals targeted were potentially boundless. It was also possibly everlasting, since the conditions for ending it – the defeat of every terrorist group of global reach – were unachievable. These terms of conflict have had important implications for the treatment of designated enemies. Recall that suspects in peacetime must be tried and charged, while combatants detained from a battlefield may be held until the end of hostilities. What counts as a battlefield if the whole world constitutes the theatre of operations? And what counts as the end of hostilities if the war is perpetual?

The Geneva Conventions recognize individuals as either combatants or civilians, each with corresponding rights:

> Every person in enemy hands must have some status under international law: he is either a prisoner of war and, as such, covered by the Third Convention, a civilian covered by the Fourth Convention, or again, a member of the medical personnel of the armed forces who is covered by the First Convention. There is no intermediate status; nobody in enemy hands can be outside the law.[19]

The definition of all those captured in the war on terror as 'enemy combatants', undeserving of the treatment usually granted to prisoners of war, has allowed detainees to be held without trial or charge for decades. The most famous detention site is Guantánamo Bay, the military prison on Cuba which operates externally to the domestic jurisdiction of the US and in which prisoners are held in legal limbo: outside of international human rights law and domestic law, in indefinite military detention (as if they were prisoners-of-war [POWs]) but without any of the legal protections that POWs are afforded. Approximately

780 detainees have passed through Guantánamo since 2002 (including several children under the age of 18), and have been held for months, years and sometimes decades. As of August 2023, 30 people remain in the prison, 11 of whom have been charged with war crimes in the military commissions system (one person convicted and ten awaiting trial) and 16 who have been cleared for release but are still detained. The remaining three are held in indefinite detention, neither facing charges nor recommended for release.[20]

The military commissions were established through a Military Order issued by Bush on 13 November 2001, which allowed detainees to be tried outside of the US's federal courts system. Following the 2006 *Hamdan* v. *Rumsfeld* Supreme Court case, which found that the commissions violated the Geneva Conventions, an act was passed in Congress (Military Commissions Act of 2006, amended in 2009) to allow them to continue. However, the commissions remain controversial and legal scholars have argued that they are seriously flawed in their ability to provide fair trials for those accused, noting that there are no genuine rules of evidence, no guidance on how questions of admissibility of evidence should be dealt with and no form of genuine appeal. As one lawyer working on these cases noted, the commissions effectively make the US Executive 'captor, jailer, prosecutor, defender, judge of fact, judge of law and sentencer with no appeal to an impartial and independent judicial body'.[21]

Aside from the issue of fair trials, the use of the 'enemy combatant' label has been most troubling in its subversion of international norms on the treatment of detainees, both inside Guantánamo and in the custody of Central Intelligence Agency (CIA) officials at numerous secret prisons or 'black sites' across the world prior to their arrival in Cuba. Abuses in armed conflict are, unfortunately, frequent. This is why a set of laws governing the treatment of detained adversaries has been developed over time: in international humanitarian law (via the 1949 Geneva Conventions, and their Additional Protocols [1977]); international criminal law (via the 1998 Rome Statute of the International Criminal Court, which regards torture as a war crime and a crime against humanity); and international human rights law (via the 1948 Universal Declaration of Human Rights, and the 1984 UN Convention against Torture and Other Cruel, Inhuman or Degrading Treatment or Punishment [CAT]). These all provide clear prohibitions on torture and cruel, inhuman or degrading treatment.

What is notable about hybrid counterterrorism is not that torture has been used (as will be discussed in Chapter 3, it has been frequently revived in previous counterterrorism campaigns), but, rather, the way that it was justified through legal opinion at the highest levels. The CAT does not leave any room for interpretation as to what constitutes torture, defining it as 'any act by which severe pain or suffering, whether physical or mental, is intentionally inflicted on a person for such purposes as obtaining from him or a third person information or a confession'.[22] Yet, the Bush administration developed extensive legal arguments to rationalize and justify it, most notably in the 2002 'Torture Memos', which laid out a set of 'enhanced interrogation techniques' (including waterboarding, stress positions, throwing detainees against walls, confinement boxes and sleep deprivation), and argued that these did not meet the definition of torture as laid out in the CAT. Jay Bybee, Assistant Attorney General at the Office of Legal Counsel, argued that:

> [T]orture is not the mere infliction of pain and suffering on another, but is instead a step well removed. The victim must experience intense pain or suffering of the kind that is equivalent to the pain that would be associated with serious physical injury so severe that death, organ failure, or permanent damage resulting in a loss of significant body function will likely result.[23]

Through such legal gymnastics, a system of what Rebecca Sanders calls 'plausible legality' was put in place via the Torture Memos.[24] Rather than refraining from or denying torture, loopholes were identified to provide legal cover for interrogation practices. Although the memos were retracted in 2004, the damage done has been significant. On coming into office, the Obama administration publicly denounced enhanced interrogation techniques and signed into law a mandate that required all government interrogations to comply with the US Army Field Manual. However, there have been no prosecutions of those involved in torture. The implications of this are discussed in Chapter 4, but it is important to note that the legacy of these practices has had profound impacts on global counterterrorism and the US's reputation and claims to global moral leadership.

Figure 2.2: 'Torture Memo' draft, written by Deputy Assistant Attorney General John Yoo and Special Counsel Robert J. Delahunty, 9 January 2002

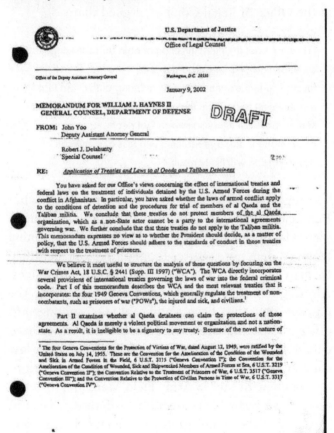

U.S. Department of Justice

Office of Legal Counsel

Office of the Deputy Assistant Attorney General   *Washington, D.C. 20530*

January 9, 2002

MEMORANDUM FOR WILLIAM J. HAYNES II
GENERAL COUNSEL, DEPARTMENT OF DEFENSE

DRAFT

FROM: John Yoo
       Deputy Assistant Attorney General

      Robert J. Delahunty
      Special Counsel

RE: *Application of Treaties and Laws to al Qaeda and Taliban Detainees*

You have asked for our Office's views concerning the effect of international treaties and federal laws on the treatment of individuals detained by the U.S. Armed Forces during the conflict in Afghanistan. In particular, you have asked whether the laws of armed conflict apply to the conditions of detention and the procedures for trial of members of al Qaeda and the Taliban militia. We conclude that these treaties do not protect members of the al Qaeda organization, which as a non-State actor cannot be a party to the international agreements governing war. We further conclude that that these treaties do not apply to the Taliban militia. This memorandum expresses no view as to whether the President should decide, as a matter of policy, that the U.S. Armed Forces should adhere to the standards of conduct in those treaties with respect to the treatment of prisoners.

We believe it most useful to structure the analysis of these questions by focusing on the War Crimes Act, 18 U.S.C. § 2441 (Supp. III 1997) ("WCA"). The WCA directly incorporates several provisions of international treaties governing the laws of war into the federal criminal code. Part I of this memorandum describes the WCA and the most relevant treaties that it incorporates: the four 1949 Geneva Conventions, which generally regulate the treatment of non-combatants, such as prisoners of war ("POWs"), the injured and sick, and civilians.[1]

Part II examines whether al Qaeda detainees can claim the protections of these agreements. Al Qaeda is merely a violent political movement or organization and not a nation-state. As a result, it is ineligible to be a signatory to any treaty. Because of the novel nature of

---
[1] The four Geneva Conventions for the Protection of Victims of War, dated August 12, 1949, were ratified by the United States on July 14, 1955. These are the Convention for the Amelioration of the Condition of the Wounded and Sick in Armed Forces in the Field, 6 U.S.T. 3115 ("Geneva Convention I"); the Convention for the Amelioration of the Condition of Wounded, Sick and Shipwrecked Members of Armed Forces at Sea, 6 U.S.T. 3219 ("Geneva Convention II"); the Convention Relative to the Treatment of Prisoners of War, 6 U.S.T. 3517 ("Geneva Convention III"); and the Convention Relative to the Protection of Civilian Persons in Time of War, 6 U.S.T. 3317 ("Geneva Convention IV").

The US was not alone in its use of torture for counterterrorism. Other states have been implicated in these practices, including European countries, which facilitated extraordinary rendition through the abduction of suspected terrorists and their transfer to black sites in the Middle East and Asia for torture. The CIA's Rendition, Detention and Interrogation programme was in place from 2001 to 2009 and involved the kidnapping, detention and torture of suspected terrorists, with at least 119 people passing through this system and the active cooperation of 40 foreign governments.[25] CIA detention sites were hosted in several European countries including Poland, Macedonia, Romania and Lithuania, and intelligence agencies, including Britain's MI5 and MI6, allegedly colluded in torture by passing on questions to interrogators at these black sites. In other cases, secret services aided the kidnapping and rendition of suspects to be tortured elsewhere. For example, the Italian military intelligence agency, Servizio informazioni e sicurezza militare, was involved in the 2003 CIA abduction of an Egyptian imam Hassan Mustafa Osama Nasr (Abu Omar), who was kidnapped in Milan and rendered to Egypt, where he was tortured and detained for four years before being released. Britain's MI6 colluded in the 2004 rendition of anti-Gaddafi dissident Abdel Hakim Belhaj and his wife Fatima Boudchar from Thailand to Libya, where they were imprisoned and tortured. And Kenyan security forces have been extensively criticized for the use of rendition and torture against terrorist suspects, including around 150 refugees who entered after the 2006 Ethiopian invasion of Somalia and were detained, vetted by US and Kenyan investigators and transferred via the Ethiopian military in Mogadishu to 'Africa's Guantánamo' in Addis Ababa.[26] Such approaches have undermined the laws governing the conduct of war and routinized human rights violations.

Given its central role in the military prosecution of the war on terror, the US was primarily responsible for muddying the waters of the laws governing international armed conflict through its hybrid approach to counterterrorism. However, hybrid counterterrorism is not fought only in the international arena. Domestic counterterrorism, which had previously largely relied on criminal justice approaches, increasingly incorporated hybrid means, blurring the boundaries between war and criminal justice and undermining long-standing norms in the process.

Due process and the domestic rule of law

Due process long pre-dates liberal democracy and it is central to written and unwritten constitutions in many states. In 1215, the Magna Carta famously set out the principles of liberty and justice that underpin the due process of the law:

> No free man shall be seized or imprisoned, or stripped of his rights or possessions, or outlawed or exiled, or deprived of his standing in any other way, nor will we proceed with force against him, or send others to do so,

except by the lawful judgment of his equals or by the law
of the land.[27]

These ideas of the need to protect individual freedom
against the excesses of government were mirrored
in the French Declaration of the Rights of Man
(1789), the Fifth and Fourteenth Amendments to the
US Constitution (the Bill of Rights, 1791) and the
Universal Declaration of Human Rights (1948).

Hybrid counterterrorism in the domestic arena has
been embraced by many states, which have created
exceptions for the specific crime of terrorism and sought
to prevent it in ways that impact on due process norms,
creating a second tier of quasi-judicial process which
operates in a pre-crime space to pre-empt individuals
and groups before they act. These new powers have
eroded established legal protections within the criminal
justice system, including *habeas corpus* (the right not
to be unlawfully or indefinitely detained), the right to
silence, presumption of innocence and access to legal
counsel. At the same time, special court proceedings
have been created for dealing with terrorism, along
with new regimes of preventative detention, intrusive
forms of surveillance, and the policing of speech
and association.

The justification for these new powers is usually
articulated through the need to balance liberty and
security. Viewed through this prism, civil liberties
provide advantages to those plotting terrorism, as they
can move uninterrupted through freer societies and
place civilians in danger. While authoritarian societies

frequently abuse rights of due process to secure the regime and are therefore assumed to be both willing and able to bolster security through anti-democratic means, liberal democracies are often understood to be particularly vulnerable due to their open nature. Both the US Secretary of Justice, John Ashcroft, and the UK Home Secretary, David Blunkett, argued in 2004 that terrorists were taking advantage of open societies and claimed that stronger security measures were needed to close the loopholes.[28]

To prevent exploitation of the freedoms within liberal democratic societies, preventative detention has become a central feature of counterterrorism in a number of states, including the UK, Australia, Canada, Germany, France, Ireland, Greece, Italy and Spain. While they vary in terms of the length of detention permitted, such laws allow the holding of a person not under arrest for several days or weeks without access, or with diminished access, to legal counsel. In the UK, for example, the Terrorism Act 2006 originally allowed for suspects to be held in pre-charge detention for 28 days, since reduced to 14 days (the ordinary limit is 24 hours). Other restrictions to due process include the use of special courts and procedures, such as secret evidence and limitations on the defence. In Australia, a 2004 law enabled the Attorney General to issue a certificate allowing the exercise of a veto over material presented to the court (including witnesses and evidence) during any trial that potentially involved matters of national security, effectively making them closed hearings.[29] Changes such as these suspend the normal rights of defendants during a criminal trial, placing trials in the hands of the executive and politicizing the criminal justice system.[30]

Long-standing due process norms have also been eroded through new understandings of prevention as the central mode of countering terrorism before it happens. This includes control orders, the institution of broad regimes of surveillance and counterextremism programmes designed to prevent people being 'drawn into' terrorism. The focus on prevention through counterterrorism means that authorities are increasingly operating on the basis of probabilities of what individuals *might* do, rather than punishing crimes that have been committed. France, in particular, has been criticized by human rights groups for its imposition of administrative control measures. Under the state of emergency, instituted in 2015 and extended six times, and later under the November 2017 'Strengthening Internal Security and the Fight Against Terrorism' law, French control measures allowed the Ministry of Interior to impose restrictions on those believed to be 'radicalized' and assign them residency in particular locations, with curfews, prohibitions on travel outside the municipality, and the requirement to report regularly to a police station.

These changes to domestic approaches to terrorism have led to what some scholars have called a 'culture of control', characterized by broad programmes of information gathering and repression, particularly of minorities.[31] For example, the charge of terrorism has been used in China to justify the repression of religious expression of Uyghur Muslims in Xinjiang and enabled it to tighten its grip on the region. Prevention is a key part of Chinese counterterrorism and includes programmes such as the 'bonding as relatives' initiative, where Han Chinese (China's dominant ethnic group) are assigned to stay in the homes of Uyghurs to 'guide their conduct' and foster 'inter-ethnic harmony', as well as 're-education programmes' that aim to transform potential radicals into productive citizens.[32] In Saudi Arabia, counterterrorism strategies such as the Intellectual Security Program and the rehabilitation programme have been developed that seek to win 'hearts and minds' through religious discourse that views terrorism as the work of those who have 'deviated' from Islam and obedience to the ruler. Through extensive counter-radicalization programmes, these 'deviants' are guided towards 'correction of thought' through the intervention of religious leaders who aim at ideological de-programming and total repentance. Those who do not repent are placed outside of the law, a status that removes all their rights, allowing for targeted killing and indefinite imprisonment.[33]

Preventative programmes have been instituted in liberal states as well, one of the most established being the UK's Prevent programme. Introduced secretly in 2003, it became public in 2007 and since then has considerably broadened its focus. Initially concerned with preventing terrorism, it was extended in 2011 to cover all forms of 'extremism' (including non-violent forms). In 2015 huge swathes of society were notionally brought into counterterrorism work via the Prevent Duty, which required teachers, lecturers, healthcare workers and social workers to monitor and report on those in their care who showed signs of radicalization. In November 2023 government documents were leaked that revealed plans to extend the definition of extremism to include anyone who 'undermines' British institutions and values.[34] These developments demonstrate how counterterrorism powers frequently expand well beyond their original remit to identify increasingly broad populations that fall under their scope.

The culture of control is perhaps clearest in the rapid expansion of state surveillance powers. Partly due to technology's ability to collect and process vast amounts of data, new powers have been instituted on the grounds that liberties must be surrendered to ensure the security of societies. China is perhaps the state that has most enthusiastically embraced the information-gathering aspects of hybrid counterterrorism. In Xinjiang, Uyghur Muslims are controlled by vast networks of high-tech surveillance systems, including zones of control monitored by CCTV linked to police databases, and designed, in the words of Deputy Secretary of Xinjiang, Zhu Hailun, to ensure 'no cracks, no blind spots, no gaps'.[35] But, again, these measures are not confined to authoritarian states: liberal democracies have similarly welcomed technological advances that allow extensive information gathering for counterterrorism purposes. The 2013 Edward Snowden revelations exposed how counterterrorism legislation under the USA Patriot Act had enabled the National Security Agency (NSA) to collect huge amounts of data from American citizens, including phone metadata, emails, and records of internet usage and transactions. Extensive surveillance is also key to European counterterrorism approaches, including in the UK, France, Denmark and the Netherlands. The Dutch were named by Snowden as the 'Surveillance Kings of Europe', due to their subversion of legal regulations that require government agencies to ask permission of citizens to access their information. Through intelligence sharing arrangements, Dutch security services were able to request from the NSA information on citizens that they had already shared, thus swerving these legal regulations.[36]

The development of domestic counterterrorism powers has reset the balance between liberty and security in states across the world. While these developments may be less surprising in authoritarian societies, in liberal democratic states the domestic realm of law and order has been fundamentally changed by new powers that have suspended civil liberties and due process norms and altered the relationship between police, security services and citizens. Contemporary hybrid counterterrorism has an unparalleled global reach due to both technological advances and the global macrosecuritization of the war on terror. But most of these practices are not new and many have been used in previous counterterrorism campaigns because of the way terrorism has been framed at particular historical moments. The next chapter considers how we got here.

3

HOW DID WE GET HERE? A SHORT HISTORY OF COUNTERTERRORISM

D uring the early decades of the 21st century, it was common to hear political figures speak of the 'new world' ushered in by the 9/11 attacks. Prominent members of the Bush administration repeatedly claimed that the world had changed on 11 September 2001. For example, five days after the attacks Vice President Dick Cheney was already arguing that 9/11 was qualitatively different to any previous terrorist incident, that the world had shifted, and that Americans should prepare for a long war.[1] On 20 September, George W. Bush explained to a Joint Session of Congress the terms of the conflict:

> Freedom and fear are at war. The advance of human freedom – the great achievement of our time, and the great hope of every time – now depends on us. Our nation –

this generation – will lift a dark threat of violence from our people and our future. We will rally the world to this cause by our efforts, by our courage. We will not tire, we will not falter, and we will not fail. ... The course of this conflict is not known, yet its outcome is certain. Freedom and fear, justice and cruelty have always been at war, and we know that God is not neutral between them.[2]

The framing of the fight against al Qaeda (and indeed against all terrorism) as a battle between freedom and fear, good and evil, became the key narrative of the war on terror in the early 21st century, and still holds sway today. These ideas were not only widely articulated in speeches by key figures in the US and elsewhere; they also became the touchstones of counterterrorism policy, finding expression in the 2002 National Security Strategy, through which the US moved to an explicitly preventive position in relation to foreign threats. As National Security Advisor Condoleezza Rice noted in her October 2002 speech about the strategy:

The fall of the Berlin Wall and the fall of the World Trade Center were the bookends of a long transition period ... after 9/11, there is no longer any doubt that today America faces an existential threat to our security – a threat as great as any we faced during the Civil War, the so-called 'Good War', or the Cold War.[3]

The idea that al Qaeda's terrorism represented as great a threat to the US as the actual breakup of the Union, Hitler's expansionism or the nuclear-armed USSR was quite a claim. But in drawing on previous 'evil' ideologies and the 'good' wars against them, Rice (and others) alluded to two key theories about the post-Cold War world that became central to the war on terror: the end of history and the clash of civilizations.

The end of history and the clash of civilizations

In a 1989 essay, developed into a 1992 book, American political scientist Francis Fukuyama argued that the Cold War's end signalled that the final great battle of ideas was over, and a clear victory had been won for liberal democracy as the ideal form of human government. Fukuyama claimed this marked the end of history: the endpoint of ideological evolution and the universalization of Western liberal democracy.[4] The collapse of the USSR and the democratization of the former Eastern Bloc (following late 20th-century democratization waves in both Latin America and South East Asia) seemed to demonstrate the truth of this thesis. And for Fukuyama and other neoconservatives, this meant that the US had a fundamental role.

The neoconservatives represented a small but powerful voice in the early years of the George W. Bush administration, drawing on ideas of American exceptionalism to argue that US power was inherently benign since its purpose was to spread (universally desired) values of liberty and democracy.[5] Originally on the left, neoconservatives had moved rightwards in response to the perceived anti-Americanism of the anti-Vietnam War movement, developing a strong moral opposition to communism and a view that the Cold War could only be won through the application of overwhelming American power in defence of US values. The end of the Cold War apparently vindicated these ideas and was taken as proof of the necessity of American power, considered redemptive in the world because of its commitment to supposedly universal liberal principles.

In the early post-Cold War world, the neoconservatives were among the most vocal groups calling for the US to take advantage of its position as sole superpower. The Project for a New American Century (PNAC), a Washington-based neoconservative think-tank created in 1997, was key to this and Fukuyama was one of 25 signatories to PNAC's declaration of principles (as were a number of high-level Bush administration figures, including Vice President Dick Cheney, Secretary of Defense Donald Rumsfeld, Deputy Secretary of Defense Paul Wolfowitz and National Security Advisor Elliott Abrams). PNAC argued for the need to use America's new position to shape the world in a favourable way to its own interests, arguing for a foreign policy that would maintain US military dominance to promote economic and political freedom abroad. The inherent virtue and benevolence of US power, it was assumed, would mean that other states and peoples would accept its role. These ideas were very clearly articulated in the Bush Doctrine, which noted that the US found itself in a moment of opportunity and a position of great military strength that could be used to extend the benefits of freedom across the globe.[6]

A few years after Fukuyama's article was published, another political scientist, Samuel Huntington, responded with his own prophecy of the post-Cold War future. In a 1993 article and a 1996 book, he argued that now the grand ideological struggles of the 20th century were over, culture would be the primary source of conflict. In his view, 'civilizations' were the largest collectivity of human cultural identities, and he warned that conflicts would occur at their fault lines: the geographical spaces where civilizations meet. Huntington understood the clash of civilizations to be a tribal conflict on a global scale and particularly marked out the fault lines of 'Islamic civilization' in the Middle East and North Africa as sites of future conflict. Islam, he claimed, 'has bloody borders'.[7]

The 9/11 attacks appeared to many to herald the unfolding of these prophecies. While scholars had unpicked and dismissed many of these arguments, news media and commentators ran with Huntington's key themes. Since the perpetrators of the attacks were not acting on behalf of a nation, Islamic 'civilization' was charged and forensically examined by those who sought to understand the reasons behind them. In the aftermath of 9/11, Huntington's book, along with – tellingly – the Qur'an, topped the bestseller charts. Yet in the rush to understand the attacks, bin Laden's 1998 fatwa against 'Jews and Crusaders', which had publicly declared war on the US (citing its aggression against Muslims through the occupation of Saudi Arabia, the 1991 Gulf War and unflinching support of Israel) was widely ignored. As Bush stated: 'They hate our freedoms – our freedom of religion, our freedom of speech, our freedom to vote and assemble and disagree with each other.'[8] By employing this narrative the attacks were understood to result from 'Muslim rage' and hatred of the West, while the US could be presented as an innocent nation, attacked not because of its actions, but because of its character.[9] In his November 2001 address to the UN General Assembly, Bush drew on both the clash of civilizations and a particularly neoconservative inflection of the end of history to explain what was at stake:

> Civilization, itself, the civilization we share, is threatened. History will record our response, and judge or justify every nation in this hall. The civilized world is now responding. We act to defend ourselves and deliver our children from a future of fear. ... As I've told the American people, freedom and fear are at war. We face enemies that hate not our policies, but our existence; the tolerance of openness and creative culture that defines us. But the outcome of this conflict is certain: There is a current in history and it runs toward freedom.[10]

In drawing the world into a global war on terror, the US had apparently found the enemy it had been lacking in the post-Cold War years, enabling high-level officials to link the past with the present in a narrative of good versus evil, where Islamist terrorism was presented as the enemy of all 'civilized' nations and American missionary exceptionalism was declared the means to conquer it.

This framing of the war on terror was central to the response that followed and the hybrid approach that has come to define counterterrorism in the 21st century. Yet the representation of terrorism as an existential threat to the state and world order has been historically commonplace. Since the emergence of anarchist terrorism in the late 19th century, through the anti-colonial, separatist and revolutionary left campaigns of the 20th century, the image of the terrorist as the embodiment of chaos, nihilism and barbarism has constantly re-emerged. Alongside these potent images, the counterterrorist has been portrayed as the last bastion of civilization against the forces of disorder, obliged to do morally questionable things for a greater good and a higher cause.

The Black International: 'anarchist' terrorism

In the late 19th century, young men and women in clandestine and loosely networked groups engaged in high-profile and daring acts of symbolic destruction – so-called Propaganda of the Deed – designed to eliminate political leaders, inspire followers and wake the masses from their slumbers to demand economic and political change. These revolutionary individuals and groups came to be lumped together under the label 'anarchist', although few of those engaging in terrorism described themselves as such and perhaps even fewer self-professed anarchists viewed terrorism as a legitimate weapon.

Anarchist terrorism, from the 1870s to the First World War, has been called the first wave of modern

global terrorism,[11] and was notable for its methods
of dynamite throwing and assassination and its goal
of the overthrow of despotic and inequitable regimes.
The assassination of Tsar Alexander II of Russia in
1881 by Narodnaya Volya (People's Will, not an
anarchist group) inaugurated the 'Decade of Regicide'
from 1892, during which more monarchs and heads
of state were assassinated than at any time in history,
including French President Sadi Carnot in 1894,
Prime Minister Antonio Canovas of Spain in 1897,
Empress Elisabeth of Austria in 1898, King Umberto
of Italy in 1900 and US President William McKinley

Figure 3.1: Aroused! Louis Dalrymple. Illustration from *Puck*, 11 July 1894

The illustration shows French President Marie François Sadi Carnot lying in state
after being assassinated by an Italian anarchist.

in 1901.[12] These political murders of leaders, often on foreign soil by international actors, shook 19th-century society, but more alarming were the apparently random attacks on civilians, including the 1886 Haymarket bombings in Chicago, the 1894 bombing at Paris's Café Terminus, the 1893 bombing of the Barcelona Opera House and the 1896 Corpus Christi procession attack in Barcelona.

The similarity in tactics of the dynamiters led to a widespread view that these acts were linked together in a vast worldwide conspiracy. These ideas were nourished by the rise of the mass media in the form of cheap, sensationalist newspapers that amplified the threat of a sinister Black International, such as the daily columns published in *The Times* ('The Anarchists') and the *London Evening News* ('Dynamiters') among others, which reported on the activities, trials and punishments of anarchists across the world. Portraying them as immoral lunatics and deranged beasts, news media linked disparate acts together as emanating from a grand plot to overthrow order, and the idea that these activities were centrally directed became so powerful that any act of assassination or bomb throwing was attributed to an anarchist plan to destroy civilization, irrespective of the perpetrator's actual ideology. The image of the anarchist prevalent at this time is well summed up in President Roosevelt's December 1901 address to Congress after the assassination of President William McKinley. Roosevelt described the anarchist everywhere as 'the deadly foe of liberty' and, in a foreshadowing of the post-9/11 language of Bush, asserted that the attack was not just against the US, but against the world:

> The blow was aimed not at this President, but at all Presidents; at every symbol of government. ... Anarchy is a crime against the whole human race; and all mankind should band against the anarchist. His crime should be made an offense against the law of nations, like piracy and that form of man-stealing known as the slave trade; for it is of far blacker infamy than either.[13]

Representing anarchists as the enemy of humanity and their violence as directed by a huge clandestine international organization had obvious advantages, and several states responded by reviving torture, undermining the rule of law, abandoning fair trials, dissolving labour organizations and suppressing left-wing publications, organizations and associations.

Attempts to assassinate Kaiser Wilhelm I in May and June of 1878, for example, offered a useful opportunity for Chancellor Bismarck to enact the Anti-Socialist Laws, designed to undermine the strength of the German Social Democratic Party by banning socialist groups, suppressing newspapers, outlawing trade unions, and arresting and deporting anarchists and socialists.[14] France's response to the December 1893 bomb attack on the Chamber of Deputies was similar, resulting in the swift enactment of the three *lois scélérates* (heinous laws). The first law was passed only two days after the bombing and criminalized 'advocacy' of any crime, condemning anyone involved directly or indirectly in

Propaganda of the Deed and enabling the widespread suppression of anarchist publications, the repression of groups (labelled 'associations of evil-doers'), the suspension of jury trials for those accused of provoking acts of violence and a news blackout on anarchist trial proceedings.[15] The most notorious response to terrorism emerged in Russia, where attempts to assassinate Tsar Alexander III led to the reversal of constitutional reforms, the elimination of jury trials and the creation of the Okhrana, a notorious secret police force, which instituted intensive surveillance of anarchists and planted spies and *agents provocateurs* in revolutionary groups in Russia and elsewhere.[16]

Since anarchist groups were naturally clandestine, evidence of involvement was scarce, and a number of states turned to torture in order to extract confessions. Despite the 1814 abolition of torture in Spain, the Barcelona Corpus Christi procession bombing in June 1896, which killed 12 and injured more than 60, led Spanish police to revive the practice. Four hundred anarchists and suspected sympathizers were rounded up, imprisoned in Montjuïc Castle fortress and subjected to beatings with rods, brandings with hot irons, the ripping out of fingernails and the crushing of testicles in order to extract confessions.[17] These reflexive overreactions sparked their own revenge attacks. Italian anarchist Michele Angiolillo assassinated the Spanish Prime Minister, Antonio Cánovas del Castillo, in August 1897 to avenge the treatment of suspected anarchists in the Montjuïc. Similarly, in France the execution of bomber François

Ravachol led to reprisals, including the 1894 bombing of Café Terminus in Paris by Émile Henry.

As repression of suspected anarchists (along with the left more generally) had little effect, states increasingly looked to international cooperation to deal with the threat. The Rome Conference was called by German Chancellor Bismarck in 1898 after the fatal stabbing of Empress Elisabeth of Austria by an Italian anarchist in Geneva. The conference aimed to produce a definition of anarchism, an agreement on prosecution and stricter border control to prevent anarchists slipping in and out of countries undetected, along with a promise that every signatory country would keep anarchists under strict surveillance and share information with one another.[18] Six years later an international meeting in St Petersburg was held, where representatives from Russia, Romania, Serbia, Bulgaria, the Ottoman Empire, Austria-Hungary, Germany, Denmark, Sweden and Norway signed a secret protocol to combat anarchist terrorism via the identification, expulsion and return of anarchists to their countries of origin.[19]

The First World War largely destroyed state cooperation on anti-anarchist measures and the Russian revolution in 1917 moved the attention of revolutionaries to a different model of generating social and political change (and similarly shifted the attention of states in terms of whom to fear and what to repress). By the late 1920s, anarchist attacks had all but fizzled out, but the development of responses to anarchism demonstrates well the ways that the fear and threat of terrorism led to the abandonment of the rule of law in many states. The representation of a vast and secretive terrorist menace stretching across continents led to extraordinary counterterrorism actions that revived torture, suspended ordinary judicial procedures and fair trials, enabled the creation of vast surveillance mechanisms, and criminalized and repressed freedom of thought, expression and assembly. To be sure, not every targeted state enacted all of these measures. But the near universal acceptance of anarchist terrorism as an overwhelming and imminent existential threat to civilization enabled states to justify these measures as necessary, a justification that would become very familiar over the next century.

Colonial control: the birth of counterinsurgency

The representation of anarchist terrorism as an existential threat to the civilized world was soon to be mirrored in responses to the waves of anti-colonial violence that hit European powers in the early to mid-20th century. The suspension of normal rules was again demanded to protect civilization, this time against rebellions in colonies including the Philippines, Malaya, Kenya and Algeria, where groups and individuals labelled terrorists were defined in highly racialized ways as savage and barbaric. Against these rebellions, colonial administrators demanded control of populations, through information gathering and extensive surveillance, indefinite detention without trial, and brutal practices of torture along with human rights abuses designed to break the insurgencies. It's important to note how central the discourse of civilization was to these practices. It was in these practices of countering what we now call insurgency, but which was labelled then as terrorism, that the antecedents of 21st-century counterterrorism approaches began to take shape. In order to restore order, colonial security forces relied on racist ideas of how to confront 'barbaric' uprisings against 'enlightened, civilized' powers that have fed into today's hybrid approach.

Widespread surveillance was essential to managing colonial populations and was made possible by armies of anthropologists, race scientists, and so on, who claimed to know the 'mind' of the populations over which colonial forces sought control. These developed into practices to manage civilian populations, for example, in settler colonies in Canada, Australia and New Zealand, where widespread surveillance was to distinguish 'good' from 'bad' indigenous subjects, the former being those who adapted to European values, the latter being those who resisted and threatened the settlement project.[20] The British introduced extensive fingerprinting in India as early as the 1870s and this evolved into huge projects of information collection, networks of informers, and classification of individuals according to the logic of 'telling' loyal subjects from agitators.[21] These practices were used by other colonial states including the Dutch in the East Indies and the French in Indochina and North Africa.

Algeria was colonized in the 1830s and designated as part of metropolitan France from 1848, however vast economic and political inequalities remained between *pieds-noirs* (French colonial settlers) and indigenous Algerians, the majority of whom were Muslim and whose access to citizenship and political representation required renouncing religious law. The Algerian War of Independence (1954–62) was characterized by brutal National Liberation Front terrorist attacks on *pieds-noirs* and Algerian collaborators, and a French counterinsurgency approach of colonial control and collective punishment, including extrajudicial execution, disappearances and torture. The quadrillage system was central to this. Aiming to put French soldiers among the people to win hearts and minds, it divided the country into grids to be secured under repressive surveillance and curfews. Around 1.4 million Algerians were forcibly relocated to internment camps (*centres de regroupement*) and more than 24,000 men (3,000 of whom were never heard from again) were placed in pre-emptive detention during the Battle for Algiers in 1957.[22]

Detention without trial was also a central feature of colonial counterinsurgency campaigns in British colonies. Emergency Powers allowed for the widescale detention of suspected rebels and large numbers of anti-colonial supporters were detained during the Malaya Emergency of 1948–60 and later in Kenya during the Mau Mau uprising (1952–60), where detentions were often based on little more than ethnicity or tribal connection. At the height of the Kenyan Emergency, 70,000 Kikuyu (the ethnic group associated with Mau Mau oaths, which pledged to fight for liberation from British colonizers) were detained, and an estimated

150,000 in total passed through detention camps, where human rights abuses and torture were endemic.[23]

Within detention camps, interrogation techniques involved practices designed to extract intelligence and break the will of detainees. British counterinsurgency campaigns, for example, made use of restricted diets, loud noises for long periods, stress positions and sleep deprivation.[24] Similarly, the French used torture to screen Algerian detainees to sort friend from enemy and gather intelligence through the ingurgitation of water, painful suspension, beating and electric shocks.[25] These practices were not limited to the European powers, and the 'water cure' was a form of torture used frequently by American colonial police in the Philippines during the first decades of the 20th century:

> The victim was bound or otherwise secured in a prone
> position; and water was forced through his mouth
> and nostrils into his lungs and stomach until he lost
> consciousness. Pressure was then applied, sometimes by
> jumping upon his abdomen to force the water out. The
> usual practice was to revive the victim and successively
> repeat the process.[26]

The legality of this method was debated even at this time. Edwin Glenn was court-martialled in 1902 for his role in using the illegal interrogation method of the 'water cure' against Filipinos (although he received only a US$50 fine).

Illiberal coercive practices were used relatively freely in the colonies partly because of racist ideas of how

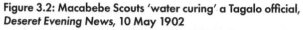

Figure 3.2: Macabebe Scouts 'water curing' a Tagalo official, *Deseret Evening News*, **10 May 1902**

to confront 'barbaric' uprisings and partly because colonial pacification (against subjects, rather than citizens) could take place away from public scrutiny and with relatively little in the way of checks and balances. And what was learned in the colonies was brought back home to the metropole; these approaches developed into regularized, institutionalized theories and practices of counterinsurgency. The escalation of leftist and separatist terrorism in the late 20th century led a cadre of counterterrorism experts back to the methods devised during the colonial counterinsurgency campaigns, and these still hold sway today. For example, due in a large part to the influence of John Nagl (a West Point professor, commander, and contributing editor to the Army and Marine Corp's field manual in counterinsurgency) and General David Petraeus, the British campaign in Malaya and the

French campaign in Algeria became the blueprints for US strategy in Afghanistan and Iraq.[27]

Enemies within: counterterrorism in the late 20th century

From the early 1970s, terrorism became a much more visible phenomenon as a plethora of oppositional groups emerged using spectacular terrorist events to publicize their causes on TV screens across the world. While groups with separatist or revolutionary left ideologies had been using bombs and guns, as well as hijackings, kidnappings and hostage taking, throughout the late 1960s, it was the 1972 massacre of Israeli athletes at the Munich Olympics by the Palestinian group Black September that arguably ushered in the era of international terrorism and created a corps of counterterrorism experts dedicated to its eradication.[28]

Many of the groups employing terrorism at this time were inspired by third world ideology (particularly the Chinese and Cuban revolutions) and sought independent states, while their leftist aspirations and transnational connections led many observers to believe that they were directed by the USSR. As a result, and in the context of the Cold War, they were seen as both an internal threat to society (like the anti-colonial militants) *and* a threat to the international order (like the anarchists). This understanding allowed diverse groups with various aims to be collected under the umbrella identity of transnational terrorist, viewed as the enemy within and the fomenter of global disorder. Separatist and revolutionary left groups had different, although sometimes overlapping, goals, as with Euskadi Ta Askatasuna (ETA – Basque Homeland and Freedom) and the Irish Republican Army (IRA), who ostensibly aimed for socialist states. But they employed similar tactics, often trained together, traded weapons and learned from one another. The proliferation of terrorism in the last third of the 20th century meant that counterterrorist forces were also able to observe, imitate and apply the tactics and approaches used in different theatres to their own struggles, resulting in a raft of emergency measures that treated terrorism as a special kind of violence that required extraordinary methods. Many of these, however, were not new and drew upon the same ideas about counterterrorism that had been employed in previous campaigns.

Detention was a key instrument in countering both separatist and leftist terrorism. Internment without trial had been on the statute books in Northern Ireland since the partition of the island in 1922. In August 1971 the British government used these provisions extensively in Operation Demetrius, which removed suspected Provisional IRA (PIRA) terrorists from the streets in an effort to gather intelligence, appease hard line Unionists and reduce support among nationalists through intimidation.[29] Over the next four years 1,981 people were interned without trial, the vast majority of whom had no connection to the paramilitaries. Since confessions were needed to secure convictions, the so-called 'five techniques' were used extensively on detainees. These had been imported from, and had proven useful in, Britain's early and mid-century colonial counterinsurgency campaigns, and consisted of hooding, food and water deprivation, sleep deprivation, being subjected to continuous and monotonous noise, and forcing detainees to stand against a wall with legs apart and hands above the head for several hours.

Other states made similar use of preventative detention. Following the occupation of Gaza and the West Bank in 1967, Israel instituted an extensive system of administrative detention in the Occupied Territories, a remnant of British Emergency Regulations from 1945 that allowed the Israeli Military Governor to order preventative detention of suspects without charge, trial or explanation other than 'endangering security', for periods sometimes lasting years. An estimated 800,000 Palestinians have experienced some form of detention since 1967.[30] Five methods of physical pressure were used against detainees, including shaking, the 'Shabach' position (a small, low chair, tilted forward, where the suspect was painfully shackled for long periods of time, head covered by a sack and loud music played), the 'Frog Crouch' (where the suspect was forced to crouch on the tips of toes for consecutive five-minute intervals), excessive tightening of hand or leg cuffs, and sleep deprivation.[31]

Due process was also undermined during these counterterrorism campaigns. The 1973 Northern Ireland (Emergency Provisions) Act, for example, suspended the right to trial by jury to avoid intimidation of witnesses and jurors. So-called Diplock Courts (named after Lord William Diplock, who chaired a parliamentary commission on the administration of justice in the province) were also convened, which limited both the right to silence and the right to access legal counsel in terrorism offences and tried cases before a single judge. In addition, the testimony of so-called supergrass informants was used to mitigate the problems of evidence collecting in areas where security forces were at high risk of ambush. This system allowed charges to be brought on the word of highly placed informants and by the time it ended the supergrass system had charged around 500 people on the uncorroborated word of 27 individuals. The extraordinary counterterrorism legislation in Northern Ireland produced very few convictions and was frequently used to prosecute offences other than terrorism, feeding the perception in the province that the British government was corrupt and encouraging support for the PIRA. Only slightly more than 1 per cent of all those detained between November 1974 and February 2001 were actually charged with a terrorism offence.[32]

In Latin America in the 1970s and 1980s, the fear of a Cuban-style revolution encouraged the view that left-wing movements were part of a worldwide communist conspiracy, and a number of states empowered military and paramilitary forces to use brutal repression to defeat those they deemed terrorists. Those suspected of belonging to the Maoist Tupamaro group in Uruguay, for example, were subjected to systematic beatings and electrocution in police stations even before the democracy was crushed. Once the government gave the military a 'blank cheque' to defeat the group, it duly did so through the application of overwhelming armed force, and a year later (in 1973) went on to overthrow the democratic government.[33] Colombia attempted to combat the far-left M-19 urban guerrilla movement using new laws introduced under the National Security Statute (1978–82), which resulted in the arrest of 60,000 Colombians (for subversive activity), widespread torture, and the assassination of more than 1,000 individuals.[34] In Brazil, the idea of the leftist enemy within was long-standing and, when the military seized power in 1964, the Doctrine of National Security was created, instituting an internal war which aimed to root out the Ação Libertadora Nacional. In 1968 an Institutional Act was passed that aimed to prevent 'revolutionary war' through the suspension of *habeas corpus* for political crimes and crimes against 'national security', as well as widespread repression of oppositional groups and the disappearance and killing of those suspected of being involved with or sympathetic to militant groups.[35] Paramilitary forces were central to the counterterrorism strategies in Latin American dictatorships. In Argentina, the Peronist-created Argentine Anti-Communist Alliance (Triple A) was instituted in 1973 from a mix of police, soldiers and thugs to undertake kidnapping, torture and assassination of suspected leftists. This activity was later extended by the dictatorship in its Dirty War (1974–83) in which around 30,000 people were kidnapped, tortured and murdered. As elsewhere, Argentina's Dirty War modelled its methods on French counterinsurgency in Algeria, turning the power of the state on the enemy within. As de facto President Jorge Videla, appointed in 1976 by the military junta, noted, the repression was directed against those not considered Argentine: 'Those whose ideas are contrary to our Western, Christian civilization.'[36]

While the Latin American dictatorships were relatively open in their use of extrajudicial means to pursue those labelled terrorists, democracies also killed suspected terrorists and set up paramilitary groups. Israel has employed a clandestine programme of assassination since the state's birth, targeting fugitive Nazi war criminals and Arab and Iranian nuclear and other scientists, as well as Palestinian militants. Following the Munich Olympics massacre, Operation Wrath of God was initiated to hunt down those involved and 'terrorize the terrorists', resulting in the assassination of several targets throughout the 1970s in Italy, France, Cyprus and Lebanon, as well as in Gaza and the West Bank.[37] The policy of targeted killing of designated terrorists remains in place today, having been officially acknowledged as state policy since the Second Intifada (2000–5). The early response to Italy's Red Brigades included the 1970s 'strategy of tension' policy, which aimed to exploit the atmosphere of extreme civil unrest to increase public demand for law-and-order measures. Through this, the Italian secret service (Servisio Informazione Democraticia [SID]) staged acts of terrorism and the training of 'counter-revolutionary' soldiers. Members of the SID were directly implicated in the Rosa dei Venti organization, which in 1974 was in the process of bringing together armed groups to stage a coup in order to re-establish a fascist government.[38] Similarly, following the Spanish transition to democracy, after the death of Franco in 1975, ETA terrorism was countered through a formal policy of conventional police work that existed alongside a covert policy of paramilitary targeting. Formed in 1983, the paramilitary Anti-terrorist Liberation Groups (GAL) were created and financed by the Ministry of the Interior of the Spanish Socialist Workers' Party in order to eliminate ETA activists. In bringing together violent far-right groups and mercenaries, the aim was to destroy ETA by eliminating its leadership, particularly in the French Basque region. By taking the battle to French territory, where ETA operatives had been tolerated, GAL's targeted killing programme aimed to generate a public outcry that would pressure the French government into greater cooperation with Spain in solving the conflict.[39] The GAL operated until 1987, engaging in abductions, torture and assassination of suspected terrorists in the Basque Country and killing 27 suspected ETA members, a third of whom had no connection to terrorism at all.[40] As with the reactionary counterterrorism measures against anarchists, this dirty war served ETA well by demonstrating its claim that the Spanish state – even democratized – was repressive and willing to suspend human rights and the rule of law in its dealings with the Basques.

The language of the enemy within had the effect of bringing a hugely diverse set of groups under one umbrella definition of 'the terrorist', constructed as a threat to civilization. Drawing on similar frames to those used to represent anarchist terrorism in the 19th century and using the counterinsurgency methods developed by the French in Algeria and the British in Malaya, practitioners of counterterrorism were portrayed as heroes forced to use unsavoury methods for a greater good.

The excesses of counterterrorism in the late 20th century demonstrate how the framing of terrorism as a threat to the civilized world leads to a parallel framing of counterterrorism as a necessary evil. The ideological motivations and tactics of groups using terrorism have been varied, but states have frequently come to the same conclusion: that in order to rescue that state from an existential threat, the state itself must resort to actions that essentially meet the definition of terrorism. Often, these methods have backfired, creating counterproductive results, including an upsurge in membership and support for the groups defined as terrorist (as with the PIRA following Operation Demetrius) and a broadening of security operations that inevitably caught innocent people in its net (as in the colonial campaigns in Kenya and Algeria and the disappearances in Argentina and Uruguay). While the dictatorships discussed here felt little need to respect the rule of law, for democracies the damage done to the legitimacy and credibility of the state was significant.

The pressure that terrorist campaigns place upon states to depart from accepted ways of operating produce legal grey zones where states of emergency provide cover for actions that would ordinarily be outside the scope of legitimate action. The introduction of these in the democratic states discussed here served to construct egregious counterterrorism approaches as necessary evils in the face of attacks on the state. But they also illustrate the difficulties of keeping security forces in check.

The claim, pervasive in the aftermath of the 9/11 attacks, that the civilized world teetered on an existential precipice is one that has been heard again and again through the history of counterterrorism. And as the framing of terrorism is familiar, so are the methods used to counter it. The tactics central to contemporary hybrid approaches have been justified in the name of civilization and dire need previously. Whether used against a shadowy Black International, a rebellious colony or an internal enemy, 'civilized' states have been willing to employ coercive, illegal and unjust practices that undermine human rights in dangerous ways in the name of securing civilization. It should also be obvious that counterterrorism approaches build on and recycle – often in deeply problematic ways – previous campaigns from within and outside the state in question. Coercive counterterrorism practices emerging from the colonial period were revived in later periods, and not just by the former colonizers. US counterterrorism programmes in Africa today (see Chapter 4) bear a striking resemblance to the 'Jakarta

Methods', programmes undertaken in the 1960s and 1970s by US-trained and -supplied military officials to crush nascent left-wing movements in developing countries, including Indonesia (where they were pioneered), Chile and Brazil, and which resulted in the murder and disappearance of hundreds of thousands of people identified as 'communist' and the establishment of right-wing authoritarian military governments.[41] Malaysia's contemporary counterterrorism legislation is built on the British 1948 Emergency Ordinance in Malaya, and both Kenya and Israel have carried forward British legislation for dealing with terrorist threats. The counterinsurgency approaches developed to tackle anti-colonial terrorism in Malaya and Kenya were later used by the British in Northern Ireland, French methods were exported for use in Latin American counterterrorism in the 1970s and 1980s, and both British and French models were rediscovered and revived during the war on terror.

Given the history of violent counterterrorism practices, what is different about the hybrid model? Arguably the difference lies in the efforts made to justify these practices as reasonable policy responses to deal with those designated as terrorists. As noted in the previous chapter, under the war on terror the US in particular has argued for the legality of practices like preventative detention and torture, as well as the need for the suspension of due process, and these arguments have subsequently been adopted elsewhere. Rather than overtly violating laws (as in Latin American dictatorships) or covering up abuses (as in colonial Kenya and the Philippines), the hybrid model attempts to legitimize these through legal argument. If extraordinary measures can be rationalized through claims that they meet international norms regarding the rule of law, however tenuously, then international law can serve as a justification for these practices. This explains the attempts in the 21st century to construct legal arguments about the legitimacy of preventive war, targeted killing, torture and indefinite detention. States are required to make these arguments because their use of these practices must be accepted as (at least partially) legitimate by audiences, including public, other states and international bodies.

And this is what is so troubling and potentially damaging about hybrid counterterrorism. The practices, to be sure, are not new and the justifications for using them are also familiar. What is novel is that these practices are not only relatively open, but they are legitimated through claims that they are – despite appearances – within the norms of acceptability. International norms operate as constraints that force states to justify their actions. But in explaining their counterterrorism practice through dubious interpretations, international law has been used (and, I would argue, abused) by states as a means through which to institute, embed and diffuse their own interpretations of what the law allows.[42] These counterterrorism practices have important consequences, for the identities of states themselves and the lives of those within them and those outside. The following chapter considers the problems of hybrid counterterrorism.

4

THE PROBLEMS OF COUNTERTERRORISM

Hybrid counterterrorism approaches that blur the line between war and criminal justice to introduce powers like widespread surveillance, targeted killing, indefinite detention and torture arguably have some tactical advantages for the states that employ them. By taking potential and suspected terrorists off the streets and disrupting plots, these methods appear to prevent imminent attacks and thus be beneficial in countering terrorism (although there is considerable disagreement about this). It is less clear whether there are longer-term strategic benefits to these approaches, particularly when we consider the potential damage done to the legitimacy of the states using them. Given the extensive human and financial resources that go into counterterrorism, not to mention the post-9/11 changes to domestic and international laws and norms, we need to ask whether the efforts invested have produced results. Are these practices actually working to counter terrorism? This chapter discusses three key problems of contemporary counterterrorism: that its effectiveness is questionable; that it is frequently counterproductive; and that its erosion of domestic and global norms undermines the security of civilians and the stability of the international order.

Is counterterrorism effective?

Since 2001 counterterrorism has boomed. The leading spender by far has been the United States, and the post-9/11 wars alone have cost the US in excess of US$8 trillion,[1] not including the economic costs of domestic counterterrorism measures, which were estimated to have reached US$78.6 billion in 2018.[2] Counterterrorism spending across the world is difficult to measure because states are rarely transparent about it and may count a wide variety of expenditures (including military spending, counter-radicalization programmes and police activities) under this umbrella. Nevertheless, indicators show that counterterrorism activities receive incredibly large proportions of domestic and international funding. Nigeria, for example, spent more than US$8.5 billion on its counterterrorism programmes from 2010 to 2017, and EU expenditures totalled US$4.4 billion between 2014 and 2020 (not including Europol and counter-radicalization programmes).

These figures illustrate the significant sums sunk into counterterrorism today. Yet, despite the immense financial and human resources that underpin them, the effectiveness of these programmes is, at best, unclear. This partly stems from a lack of clarity as to what successful counterterrorism looks like. Is the desired outcome a reduction in terrorist attacks? A reduction in terrorist plots? An acceptable level of terrorist threat? A functioning society and economy? A widespread sense of security within the population of a state? Or a more cohesive society that does not breed grievances? If the aim is to reduce terrorism, then our unit of measurement is something that *does not* happen, and it is not clear whether we should be measuring this in negative terms (fewer or no terrorist attacks) or in positive terms (a more ideal democratic society with fewer grievances and fewer reasons for violent opposition).[3] It may be possible to entirely eradicate terrorism in a totalitarian society, but would this really constitute a counterterrorism victory? Most people would agree that this would amount to state terrorism and would in fact create grievances that could (and likely inevitably would) spill over eventually into terrorist acts against the government.

Since the objective of terrorism is to cause fear in a society to force political change, perhaps our gauge should be how safe and secure people feel. Counterterrorism could then be judged effective if the population does not live in fear of terrorist attacks. The problem with this measure is that fear of terrorism does not correlate well with realities on the ground, and opinion polling has demonstrated that fear of terrorism may be very high even in countries where terrorism is relatively low. In 2020, for instance, more than 86 per cent of respondents to the World Values Survey in Zimbabwe reported worrying about terrorism 'very much' or a 'great deal', even though the country experienced only 12 terrorist incidents (with a total of three fatalities and 50 injured) in the entire previous decade.[4] Similarly puzzling poll results have emerged in other countries. Despite a lengthy counterterrorism campaign abroad and extensive measures at home, 36 per cent of Americans polled in 2021 reported feeling very or somewhat worried about becoming a victim of terrorism.[5] If more than a third of Americans remain so anxious about terrorism, does this indicate that the counterterrorism measures introduced in the US have been a failure?

One variable that analysts frequently use to determine the effectiveness of counterterrorism is the number of terrorist attacks. The rationale goes that if a particular counterterrorism approach reduces the number or lethality of attacks, then it is effective. Evaluating the success of strategies using this measurement is, however, quite difficult as it is never altogether clear whether and to what extent a particular approach or set of strategies has led to a reduction in terrorism. The elimination of a specific group, for example, may well be the consequence of tough counterterrorism powers, but there may be other reasons too. Terrorist actors tend to be young and the activists in a particular group may have aged out of violent rebellion or decided to use political means to air their grievances. A specific group may have collapsed because its members have internal ideological or other quarrels, or because the cause itself is no longer relevant to members.[6]

The number of attacks is also not necessarily the best measure of the effectiveness of counterterrorism.[7] How can we be sure that increased powers or laws have actually had an effect, as opposed to other variables? In other words, how do we measure causation rather than correlation? A group, for example, may reduce the number of attacks in order to concentrate its resources on one large-scale, high-casualty spectacular attack. Conversely, an increase in terrorist attacks does not necessarily mean that a group is growing in capacity and that counterterrorism measures are ineffective. Attacks do not necessarily indicate the strength of an organization. Groups in decline may initiate attacks to signal that they are still relevant and leadership transitions frequently result in the radicalization of organizations. For example, the Real IRA's (RIRA) Omagh bombing in August 1998, nine months after the signing of the Good Friday Agreement, represented the largest loss of life in a single incident in Northern Ireland, killing 29 people and injuring 220. But the bombing resulted in significant backlash and the draining of both membership and support, weakening the movement and leading to the declaration of a ceasefire shortly after.[8] While counterterrorism powers, including new legislation, did have an influence on the RIRA's decline, internal debates within the group were clearly relevant and perhaps more so. And while the attack may have been an operational success, its political impact was disastrous, considerably eroding support for the RIRA within its target constituencies.

Similarly, operational counterterrorism successes do not necessarily translate into political successes, or indeed into reductions in terrorism. The sweeping arrests made in Northern Ireland during Operation Demetrius in August 1971 succeeded in taking more than 340 suspected Provisional IRA (PIRA) terrorists off the streets, but the backlash against internment and the interrogation practices employed led to an increase in both membership of the PIRA and political violence in the province.[9] Similarly, the arrest and incarceration in solitary confinement of the Germany's Red Army Faction leadership in 1972 could be deemed a counterterrorism success in the short term. However, a second wave of militants emerged in the mid-1970s to replace them.

Deciding whether to measure effectiveness in the short or long term impacts on our assessments of whether particular approaches work or not. For example, the Obama administration's drone campaign in Pakistan's Federally Administered Tribal Areas (FATA) may be seen as more or less successful depending on how we measure this. Several al Qaeda militants were indeed killed in these operations and some scholars have noted a reduction in terrorist attacks immediately after drone strikes. By these measures, the campaign should be counted a success. However, others have assessed it much less positively, pointing to the deterioration of US–Pakistan relations, the undermining of Pakistani governmental authority within its own sovereign territory, the number of civilian casualties and the continuation of al Qaeda's operational capacity over the long term.[10]

The effectiveness of counterterrorism is also difficult to measure because particular approaches may lead to substitution effects. The introduction of passenger screening in airports to prevent airplane hijackings in the 1970s, for example, did reduce the frequency of this particular terrorist tactic, but other types of attack proliferated. The border wall in Israel reduced the number of suicide attacks from the West Bank during the Second Intifada, but rocket and mortar attacks continued. Also, geographical substitution effects may result as militants move from one theatre to another to avoid counterterrorism measures. Chechen guerrillas' efforts to avoid repressive Russian counterinsurgency tactics in the early 2000s, for example, led to displacement activities which shifted the targets of terrorist operations from strikes on Russian forces in Chechnya to attacks in neighbouring republics Dagestan, Ingushetia, North Ossetia and Kabardino-Balkaria, as well as within Russia itself. This emphasizes the problem of how to assess success. Should we be measuring the reduction of the *capacity* to attack or a reduction of the *will* to attack? These questions also indicate the problems with measuring short-term (as opposed to long-term) effectiveness.

Finally, however we measure effectiveness, it is still prudent to consider whether the large sums of money spent on counterterrorism are proportional. If the costs are not proportional to the risk posed by

Figure 4.1: Israeli West Bank Barrier, north of Meitar, May 2006

terrorism, then there is a danger that vital funds are being diverted from other, more significant, risks. The post-9/11 absorption of the Federal Emergency Management Agency into the US Department of Homeland Security, for example, meant that funding for natural disaster management directly competed with counterterrorism programmes. By 2005 this had resulted in a nationwide shortfall of US$264 million for natural disaster preparedness and relief, contributing to the US government's inability to predict or mount an effective response to Hurricane Katrina, which hit New Orleans in August of that year, and resulted in more than 1,800 fatalities.[11] Researchers have undergone extensive cost–benefit analysis and risk assessment of US counterterrorism spending since 9/11, arguing that given the small probability of being killed in a terrorist attack in the US (around one in 39 million), the large expenditures would have had to save 11,797 lives per year to be justified.[12] Despite the relatively low risk of being killed in a terrorist attack, officials have continued to present terrorism as an extensive and immediate threat.

Is counterterrorism counterproductive?

Aside from the questionable effectiveness of counterterrorism, there are many reasons to believe that the practice and discourse of counterterrorism may be counterproductive. Several approaches associated with hybrid counterterrorism, including special regimes of detention and interrogation and suspension of due process, along with the targeted killing of militants, undermine long-standing human rights norms, which play into groups' grievance narratives and potentially increase recruitment. Specific practices, however, are not the only issue when considering whether counterterrorism may be counterproductive: the discourse itself should also be considered. What does it mean, for example, when leaders constantly tell the public that terrorism is an imminent and ever-present threat? Does this have the effect of, at a minimum, 'terrorizing' populations by instilling fear and changing behaviour? And at the far end of this spectrum, can the state's practice of counterterrorism in some cases itself be considered a form of terrorism?

The war on terror ushered in a range of global practices that were both legally and morally dubious, and this disregard for human rights has had far-reaching consequences in terms of the prosecution of terrorism and the possibility of justice for victims. The example of Guantánamo Bay illustrates this point. One of the key reasons it is so difficult to close the camp down (even more than a decade after President Obama signed Executive Order 13492 to do so) is that those who remain inside, including five accused of direct participation in 9/11, must be deported or tried if their cases are to be resolved. This outcome, however, has been made extremely unlikely precisely because of the counterterrorism practices used.

The Central Intelligence Agency (CIA)'s use of torture against detainees has undermined the possibility of justice being served because, under the Convention Against Torture, the evidence obtained is not admissible in court. All five of the 9/11 defendants were tortured in secret overseas CIA prisons before being transferred to Guantánamo, where they have been held without charge since. In September 2023, a military medical panel found that one of the 9/11 defendants, Ramzi bin al-Shibh (accused of organizing a cell of the hijackers), was not competent to stand trial because torture had made him severely psychotic. Al-Shibh had been held for four years at CIA black sites and was subjected to solitary confinement, sleep deprivation and cold-water treatment, leading to post-traumatic stress disorder that manifested in paranoid delusions that his Guantánamo guards were attacking him with invisible rays.[13] The use of torture (justified at the time through the Torture Memos) has thus created a situation where the 'evidence' obtained is impermissible. It is likely that the only way to close the camp, which costs around US$540 million per year to run, will be to offer the remaining prisoners plea deals. In other words, the hybrid counterterrorism measures used have brought us to a situation where some of those alleged to be responsible for 9/11 cannot be brought to justice. As retired Air Force Colonel Gary Brown, a former lawyer in the military courts system, argued, Guantánamo had 'been successful at doing something that I would have thought never could have been done, and that is generating more sympathy for the detainees'.[14]

The undermining of the potential to prosecute terrorist suspects, however, is not the only possible counterproductive effect of counterterrorism. As Andrew Silke has noted, a problem clearly exists in some form before counterterrorism measures are introduced, yet the type of measures used can profoundly influence both the nature and lethality of terrorism.[15] That violence begets more violence is often forgotten in the urge to respond to terrorism, but history shows that some counterterrorist tactics have produced counterproductive results. Increased recruitment to terrorist groups after the internment of real or perceived group members has been discussed earlier, along with the way that poorly chosen counterterrorism methods can escalate conflicts. But counterterrorism can be counterproductive even when there exists no clear terrorism threat.

For example, despite noting in the early 2000s that the region was relatively peaceful, the US has directed extensive counterterrorism assistance towards preventing the emergence of a possible Islamist threat in West Africa, particularly in Chad, Mauritania, Mali, Burkina Faso and Niger. More than US$1 billion has been distributed to the region via the Trans-Sahara Counterterrorism Partnership (TSCTP) since 2005, with the aim of strengthening counterterrorism capacity and inhibiting the spread of extremist ideology through diplomacy, development assistance and military activities.[16] Increasing counterterrorism resources in the region, however, has gone hand in hand with skyrocketing military budgets, repression of ethnic groups labelled 'jihadist' and government abuses of power. One of the flagship programmes of TSCTP is the annual exercise Flintlock, in which the US trains military personnel from member countries to strengthen cross-border collaboration in countering terrorism and providing security. As noted in Congress, Flintlock-trained officers have conducted at least five coups in the region since 2015, including against democratic governments, in Guinea (2021), twice in Mali (2020 and 2021) and twice in Burkina Faso (2015 and 2022).[17] At the same time, terrorism in the region has increased exponentially, due in no small part to the ousting of Libyan leader Gaddafi in 2011 and the instability that followed this, which allowed safe haven for militant groups and the widespread looting of regime weapons. The situation today is increasingly complex as government forces, US, European and UN soldiers, and militant separatist and jihadist groups battle one another. And the increased counterterrorism spending and powers in the region appear to be encouraging hard line approaches that themselves increase terrorism. A 2023 survey of more than 850 voluntary recruits to militant groups in sub-Saharan Africa found that of those who said a specific incident moved them to join, 32 per cent cited a particular government action and 29 per cent cited the killing of a family member or friend.[18] While the complexity of the situation means causation is difficult to trace, security in the region has clearly not been improved by the extensive counterterrorism efforts there.

Much of the contemporary debate on whether counterterrorism leads to more terrorism has focused on targeted killing. As discussed earlier, the effectiveness of taking out key members of terrorist organizations through targeted drone strikes depends on what we consider a success; it may arguably fulfil short-term objectives by removing key members with vital knowledge or ability, as well as diverting the attention and energy of militants into avoidance measures and thus diminishing their operational capacity. Proponents of drone strikes as a low-cost and low-casualty alternative to military campaigns argue that surgical strikes against terrorist groups mean that objectives can be achieved while limiting risk to military personnel or civilians. However, irrespective of whether lethal drone strikes are effective, testimony from those living in regularly targeted areas indicates that the policy is at minimum counterproductive, and potentially fulfils the criteria of state terrorism.

There is evidence that the US drone campaign in Pakistan's FATA did weaken al Qaeda in the late 2000s. For example, documents collected during the operation to kill Osama bin Laden found troves of information about the impact of targeted killing, including recommendations that leaders flee specific areas to avoid drone strikes. However, substitution effects appear to have taken place, with fighters leaving Pakistan for battlefields in Yemen, Somalia, Iraq and Syria. And as the drones followed them, the targeted killing campaign appears to have increased the ranks of militant groups in these areas. In Yemen, hundreds and perhaps thousands of tribesmen were motivated to join al Qaeda in the Arabian Peninsula due to a desire for revenge following the escalation of drone strikes.[19] The strikes also caused public outrage in Pakistan, with 2006 protests attracting 10,000 demonstrators in Karachi and around 8,000 in the FATA.[20] Although Pakistani public criticism did not appear to significantly weaken bilateral cooperation with the US, the consistent violation of sovereignty by the US in Pakistan and elsewhere served to undermine these governments' legitimacy, setting up competition between governments and militants for the loyalties of the population and damaging the perceived competence of the governments in whose territories the strikes took place.[21]

The number of civilians killed in drone strikes in counterterrorism campaigns (where the US is not openly at war, such as FATA, Yemen) is difficult to know because collecting evidence is challenging and both the counterterrorist forces and the groups targeted have incentives to respectively downplay or inflate the number of non-combatant casualties. However, discussions over the accuracy of numbers are partly a distraction from the effects of the drone campaign as a counterterrorism policy. It is not just the threat that civilians face from death and injury as a direct result of drone strikes, but the social and economic harm done to these societies that results from changes in behaviour, such as removing children from school, avoiding gatherings with others, and avoiding being outside and in particular areas. While some have claimed that the drone campaign amounts to remote-controlled repression, others have argued that the US's use of drones to combat terrorism paradoxically creates terror among civilians in the targeted area, who suffer profound psychological costs from living under constant surveillance and with the threat of injury or death.[22] This is augmented by double-tap strikes, when a further missile immediately follows an initial strike (resulting in death or injury to first responders), and signature strikes, which target based on a person's activity (such as regularly crossing borders, gathering in groups) rather than direct intelligence about who they are or what they have done. While drone strikes may well reduce terrorist attacks and lethality in the short term, the long-term effects of targeted killing as a counterterrorism policy are much less clear.

Because counterterrorism is state-directed, its targets are almost always non-state groups and individuals. This means that state terrorism itself is rarely part of counterterrorism discourse, unless the discussion is about so-called 'rogue states'. Yet, if we understand terrorism as a communicative strategy that uses violence or the threat of violence to send a message to an audience for a political purpose, then there is

Figure 4.2: Predator drone photographed at Indian Springs Auxiliary Air Field, Indian Springs, Nevada

no reason why states should be excluded from this definition. The use of targeted killing via armed drones and the effects that this has on populations in the areas targeted are particularly relevant here. Armed drones are used as a violent counterterrorism tool to protect the security of the state against far-away targets, but the knowledge that they are under constant surveillance and could be hit by a strike at any moment institutes terror as part of everyday life for those within these territories. The practice is arguably indistinguishable from terrorism itself.

Does counterterrorism undermine norms?

The tension between security and liberty is a very old problem of political theory. This tension is especially pronounced in liberal democratic states, and it is essential that the government response to terrorism does not undermine the principles of liberal democracy that underpin it. There are two key issues at stake here: first, that the state's use of excessive counterterrorist measures may pose a greater threat to liberal democracy than terrorism itself by undermining the social contract and therefore the legitimacy that the state rests upon. And, second, that the global liberal democratic order is undermined when liberal principles are set aside for the purposes of countering terrorism, with important consequences for the legitimacy of the post-Second World War international order.

The social contract and legitimacy

The historical foundation of the liberal democratic state emerged from the demand for liberty from the arbitrary will of another, and the checks and balances that exist in these states are there to protect individuals from the excesses of state power and prevent the abuse of governmental authority.[23] The principles of presumed innocence, due process and minimal force make up the legal safeguards that limit the power of those state agents permitted to use coercion against citizens, namely the police and the judiciary, and these legitimate and generate public acceptance of (limited) state violence for the purposes of safeguarding the political community. This is the social contract upon which the liberal state rests: individuals conserve their broader liberty to act as they please by giving up to the state their right to respond violently to wrongs. The state then acts on their behalf to address harms within a legal framework that relies on checks and balances to ensure that the coercive power of the state will not be turned against its own citizens. This contract relies on the understanding that the state will act fairly in its treatment of citizens. If the state does not act fairly then citizens are permitted, and perhaps required, to rise up and overthrow it.

One of the central aims of terrorism has been to provoke an overreaction from the state in order to demonstrate its illegitimacy. This was key to the actions and ideology of the Russian 'anarchists' in the 19th century and to Algerian anti-colonial militants in the 20th century, who sought to reveal the illegitimacy of Tsarism and colonialism respectively by provoking a reaction that would expose the brutality of these systems. In liberal democracies, groups have similarly used terrorism to provoke the state into suspending legal frameworks and thus show its hypocrisy and fundamental authoritarianism. A key problem for counterterrorism then is the very real need to avoid this overreaction and ensure that the rule of law is upheld. This is not just normatively necessary, in the sense that it is the right thing to do, it is also strategically necessary because the suspension of the rule of law erodes the social contract, upon which the state's very legitimacy rests.

The problem here lies in the possibility that counterterrorism measures weaken this legitimacy, undermining the trust between citizens and states by damaging liberal democratic principles in the (over) reaction to terrorism. If democratic states choose to abandon their principles in the fight against terrorism, this has significant consequences: undermining the social contract's promise of protection from arbitrary state power (by employing systematic fear in a manner similar to authoritarian states), at the same time as damaging state legitimacy through the use of extra-legal or unconstitutional measures (and feeding into challenger groups' narratives that the state is hypocritical, illegitimate and dangerous to specific groups).[24] The danger emerges from both the very real risk of violence from state practices, as well as the fear generated through counterterrorism rhetoric, where the sense of security that the state is supposed to provide is undermined by its consistent reminders that citizens are under ongoing and constant threat of terrorist attacks.

National terrorism alert systems, physical and architectural reminders of terrorist attacks (such as concrete barriers surrounding public squares, extensive airport security protocol for passengers, and so on), along with media amplification of threats work to represent terrorism as an always-present and imminent danger in everyday life. These measures can help to secure consent for state practices that require the sacrifice of liberties, but as Jessica Wolfendale has argued:

> If the state is genuinely committed to protecting citizens from the threat of terrorism, then the state has a clear duty

to demonstrate realistically the extent of the threat and how citizens can guard against it. To spread the fear of terrorism through misleading and exaggerated rhetoric is not only irresponsible but morally criticisable. If the fear that terrorism causes is one of the reasons why terrorist acts are considered morally repugnant, then to exaggerate and reinforce that fear is equally repugnant.[25]

The sense of security among citizens is not likely to be improved by spreading fear that they are constantly in danger of being attacked, and the enactment of counterterrorism measures to ensure the security of a population can paradoxically make them feel less secure. Anthony Field has called this the 'domestic security dilemma', in which the performance of state power through counterterrorism measures has the effect of making citizens feel insecure precisely because of the excessive powers their own governments claim and the possibility that these could be turned against them.[26] Field draws on the concept of the security dilemma in international relations. This is the process whereby, in seeking to defend against possible threats to national security, states build up their military defences and thus appear to other states to have offensive intentions. This leads to defensive military proliferation in those states, which, in turn, appear aggressive on the international stage and provoke further insecurity and further military build-ups. He argues that this vicious cycle can be observed not only between states but within them, as a government accumulating power generates anxiety within the population that these powers may be used to wear away liberties and oppress people within the state.

Aside from the insecurity generated among populations, counterterrorism can also directly threaten the security of citizens as sweeping powers to detain, interrogate and surveil place them at risk from state power. As noted in previous chapters, governments have historically been more than willing to extend counterterrorism powers beyond their original remit and target a broader range of people. The fears of unbridled state power to watch, interrogate and prosecute individuals are deeply associated with the totalitarian Nazi and Soviet regimes, in which state power was turned against citizens in the name of protecting some from the 'polluting' influence of others. In the 20th century, authoritarian regimes such as China, Chile under Pinochet, Argentina under the generals, Saddam Hussein's Iraq and Hosni Mubarak's Egypt have used powers to arrest, detain, torture and disappear, not only to punish or eliminate troublesome individuals, but also to generate the fear necessary to ensure compliance with the state, a fact that leads many to consider these state terrorist regimes. But within democracies, such powers have also been used. The widespread crackdown in Turkey on suspected sympathizers of the Islamic State of Iraq and Syria, for example, saw the closing down of 1,500 non-government organizations and the arrest and imprisonment of more than 80,000 people, mostly because of their alleged ties to the (anti-regime) Gülen movement.[27]

Targeted killing has also been used by liberal democratic states against their own citizens. The strike ordered by President Obama on Anwar al-Awlaki in Yemen in 2011 represented the first time a US citizen was targeted by an American drone strike (his 16-year-old son, himself a US citizen, was also killed by drone a few weeks later). The American Civil Liberties Union argued that the strike marked a worrying development if Americans could be extra-constitutionally executed by their own government without any judicial oversight.[28] Extensive power in the hands of the executive has also been noted in the case of the UK, where several dual nationals suspected of ties to terrorism have been stripped of their citizenship while abroad and in at least two cases have been subsequently killed in drone strikes. Bilal al-Berjawi and Mohammed Sakr were both killed in separate US strikes in Somalia in 2012, shortly after their British citizenship was removed, leading to concerns that the UK had effectively washed its hands of its citizens in order to allow for their extrajudicial execution by the US.

Specific groups are, of course, much more likely to be impacted by extraordinary counterterrorism measures. In Northern Ireland, Catholics were more likely to be made insecure by the state's response to terrorism because they were more likely to be caught up in its net. During the war on terror, it has been Muslims (and those perceived to be Muslim) who are most likely to be threatened by the extensive powers that states have granted themselves. This is important to note, because the existence of an Other, upon whom counterterrorism is enacted, serves to make such measures more palatable for the broader population: if they have nothing to hide, so the saying goes, they have nothing to fear. Nevertheless, the historical record does not provide comfort for those identified with the Other. As Igor Primoratz has argued, 'states have the resources and manpower to inflict far more damage on their own and other populations than any terrorist group could ever achieve'.[29]

When counterterrorism powers are introduced quickly, with little legislative scrutiny and in a state of heightened fear, the checks and balances that ordinarily exist are often swept aside. This creates an incentive for seeking broader powers while the conditions are favourable to it, as well as the possibility of mission creep. The extension of surveillance under the 2001 US Patriot Act illustrates how counterterrorism powers initially intended to target suspected terrorists frequently expand to encompass entire populations. Similar expansion has happened elsewhere, including in the UK, where the Regulation of Investigatory Powers Act 2000 has been used against journalists who refused to reveal their sources, and in India where the Prevention of Terrorism Act 2002 (POTA) granted sweeping powers of arrest and detention that were used to prosecute ordinary crimes as well as to intimidate minorities and out-groups. Although POTA was repealed in 2004, following a human rights outcry, its provisions were incorporated as amendments to the 1967 Unlawful Activities (Prevention) Act (UAPA), in

2004, 2008 and 2019. UAPA allows those investigated to be held for 180 days before charges are filed and has been used against activists, journalists and academics perceived to hold views contrary to the government.[30]

Finally, the expansion of counterterrorism powers and their use within the state may also be seen in the increasing militarization of domestic police forces, which themselves put citizens at risk from state power. In the US, the 1033 Program, created in 1996, has transferred billions of dollars of military equipment to domestic police forces, including mine-resistant vehicles, armed drones and body armour. Obama-era programmes to employ Iraq and Afghanistan veterans in law enforcement and Israeli counterterrorism training programmes for US police have arguably encouraged a 'warrior' mindset and increasingly repressive policing, primarily of racialized and minoritized populations. Military equipment and tactics, such as armoured vehicles, tear gas and snipers, are much more likely to be used to police minorities and have been used against Black and Brown protest and dissent. For example, Mine Resistant Ambush Protected vehicles obtained through Program 1033 were used against indigenous protesters in the Standing Rock Indian Reservation in 2016, and in 2020 Predator drones were used for surveillance over Black Lives Matter protests in Minneapolis.

The state has the resources and reach far beyond the dreams of even the most committed and destructive terrorist, and liberal democratic states have demonstrated that they are willing and able to use these powers in ways that undermine the security of (some of) their citizens. This has important implications for the social contract and the legitimacy of the state itself, but counterterrorism's international scope means that we need also to consider how global norms have been impacted.

The global liberal order

In addition to the effects on liberal democracy and human and civil rights within states, counterterrorism can have significant impact on the global liberal democratic order when principles are set aside for the purposes of countering terrorism. The impacts of these measures go much further than individual states, establishing new norms of engagement that undermine long-standing ways of behaving in international politics. The issue is not so much that preventative detention, torture, targeted killing and excessive internal security measures against terrorism are practised – as noted in Chapter 3, these have long been used by states claiming to prevent terrorism. The issue is that, rather than being veiled in secrecy and plausible deniability, these measures have been open, overt and given the veneer of legitimacy through the deployment of legal opinion. As a result, international norms in place since at least the end of the Second World War have come under pressure.

Chapter 2 discussed some of the global norms that have been eroded by hybrid counterterrorism practices. These may be understood as standards of appropriate behaviour that regulate how states ought to act in the international system. We understand appropriate behaviour in any given space because inappropriate behaviour draws criticism or sanction from other actors. When actors in a given system break norms, they have to explain their actions in order to avoid or manage the stigma of norm-breaking,[31] and the existence of extensive explanations for counterterrorism measures often indicates that international norms are being broken or stretched. In the war on terror, many global norms were placed under strain by the behaviour particularly of the US, which, as a global superpower with a strong rhetorical commitment to human rights and liberal democracy, is a key actor. Its extensive efforts to explain why captives taken from battlefields in Afghanistan and Iraq were not prisoners of war but enemy combatants, and the specific instances when torture might be used (in the Torture Memos), indicate that these behaviours were contrary to international human rights and law – if they were not norm-breaking, they would not have required such extensive explanation. And if the US, as a leading liberal democratic state, can use these arguments, then it indicates that shifts may be occurring in the wider human rights and liberal democratic landscape. We find ourselves in a situation, created over the last two decades of the war on terror, where assertions that we are at war have enabled the displacement of long-standing rights, laws and obligations.[32]

Averell Schmidt and Kathryn Sikkink have argued that the undermining of norms under the hybrid model has facilitated violations by a broad range of actors. While some democratic states challenged US discourse and practice, others chastised US hypocrisy, and China, Iran, North Korea, Syria and Cuba have all argued that the US's own human rights violations make it unfit to admonish other states. Many other states have sought to validate their own actions with reference to US justifications. For example, in 2004 Sudan 'borrowed' the US concept of illegal combatants to justify its actions in Darfur. Similarly, in the aftermath of the April 2014 coup attempt in Comoros, government and military forces mirrored US war on terror language when they detained alleged militants as 'enemy combatants' and claimed that they were being subjected to 'enhanced interrogation' techniques, rather than torture.[33]

The precedents set by the increasing use of armed drones as an acceptable counterterrorism measure have also muddied the waters on extrajudicial killing both inside and outside a given state's territory. Several countries have developed armed drones as part of their counterterrorism programmes, including France, the UK, Russia, Israel, Iran, Iraq, the United Arab Emirates, Pakistan, Turkey and Nigeria. There is no reason to believe that these and future armed drone-wielding states will be circumspect in their use, especially if norms continue to be stretched. In 2013, as the US stepped up its targeted killing programme, Michael Boyle warned that lethal drones would eventually be in the hands of those with fewer scruples than President Obama.[34] The Trump administration's attack on Iranian Quds Force leader Qasem Soleimani in January 2020 arguably represented just that. The option of targeting Soleimani had been rejected by both the George W. Bush and Obama administrations but was undertaken by Trump without the checks and balances that such dramatic policy options would usually necessitate. This demonstrates the danger of a lack of established rules of engagement for the use of targeted killing of suspected terrorists and the potential for counterterrorism approaches to generate considerable insecurity in the international system by undermining long-standing norms against the assassination of state leaders in opponent regimes.

These issues indicate that we need urgently to rethink our approaches to counterterrorism, but they also highlight a key question: if counterterrorism is, as I have argued here, questionably effective and even counterproductive, why do states pour such vast amounts of human and economic energy into it?

Contemporary counterterrorism creates 'winners' just as it creates 'losers', providing material (political and economic) and non-material (ideological, psychological and cultural) benefits for a range of actors, generating some very powerful reasons for the institution and institutionalization of counterterrorism measures. Once officials are engaged in the counterterrorism enterprise, they have a strong interest in keeping it alive. Politicians may derive extensive political benefits from appearing tough on terrorism, and at the same time fear that downplaying the dangers could – should a terrorist attack happen – lead to a loss of support. A public consistently told about the dangers of terrorism through campaigns that urge them to 'see it, say it, [and get it] sorted' will continue to demand that leaders protect them. At the same time, as David Keen has noted, the aim of wars is not always to 'win' and benefits that individuals or groups may derive from conflicts (including conflicts against terrorism) include making money, the ability to carry out abuses out of plain sight, and the political and economic benefits of states of emergency.[35]

Ultimately, the key beneficiary of hybrid counterterrorism practice is the state itself. If terrorism seeks to strike at and erode the social contract, then the state seeks to respond by demonstrating that its authority remains intact. As such, the self-perpetuating cycle of terrorism and counterterrorism allows the state to continually (and never-endingly) perform its political authority through its practice of security, in order to demand recognition of this authority from inside and outside its borders and demonstrate the necessity of the state itself. But as noted here, there are numerous problems with the way counterterrorism is performed today. If we are serious about countering terrorism, and reducing it in the long term, then we need to think beyond reactive approaches and have the courage to imagine better futures.

5

WAYS FORWARD

Despite the huge cost of hybrid counterterrorism in terms of both blood and treasure, the effectiveness of this approach is questionable, it has frequently been counterproductive, and it has opened the door to grave abuses of human rights and civil liberties, which in turn have undermined liberal norms both within states and within the global order more broadly. The long shadow of the war on terror remains over counterterrorism, even after withdrawal from its key theatres and the killing of the chief architect of the 9/11 attacks, Osama bin Laden.

In the middle of the third decade of this century, it would be difficult to argue that the record showed many successes. In areas where hard counterterrorism campaigns have been fought by states, terrorism has increased. The wars fought by the US and its coalition partners in Afghanistan and Iraq created violent groups and insurgencies that employed terrorism to strike back, as did the Russian campaign in Chechnya, the

Israeli campaigns in Gaza and the West Bank, and the militarized campaigns in the Sahel. These have spilled over, with mobile militants moving from theatre to theatre, as in Yemen, Libya and Syria, bringing conflict to more regions and creating more destruction and more displaced and insecure people. And where counterterrorism campaigns have reduced terrorism within particular states, they appear to have done so at the expense of stability and security elsewhere. At the same time, countering terrorism through the extensive surveillance of populations and the militarization of police has transformed the domestic landscape of states, and increased the insecurity of vulnerable populations, including minorities, foreigners and refugees. Comparing the global picture today to that at the start of the 21st century, we are clearly not living in a more secure world.

These approaches have been made possible by the securitization of terrorism as an existential threat to the state, and when considering ways out of this predicament it is necessary to recognize that counterterrorism measures have frequently added to human suffering. If we want to alleviate this, we should be seeking to enhance human, rather than state, security. This requires a shift from the narrow focus on countering terrorism to a broader appreciation of the contexts of violence out of which terrorism emerges. This means, in the short term, a clear-sighted assessment of the extent and nature of the problem of terrorism; in the short to medium term, a more limited approach to countering it that prioritizes the rule of law and places checks and balances on executive power; and in the long term, a broader understanding of security that appreciates conflict contexts and the strategic limits of counterterrorism, as well as its counterproductive effects.

Desecuritizing terrorism

The potential for a more effective counterterrorism requires first a recognition that, irrespective of the specific ideological cause that any given group at any given moment espouses, terrorism is very unlikely to ever be eradicated. This does not mean that states should simply sit back and wait to be attacked, but it does mean recognizing that this threat, like other risks, is part of life. As a tactic used by non-state groups, terrorism aims to effect political change by generating fear and anxiety in a population, making the costs of terrorism too much to bear and causing an overreaction in the targeted state. One way of responding to this is to refuse to succumb to the anxieties that terrorism generates. As John Mueller notes: 'Since the creation of insecurity, fear, anxiety, hysteria, and overreaction is central for terrorists, they can be defeated simply by not becoming terrified and by resisting the temptation to overreact.'[1]

Counterterrorism rhetoric in the 21st century has done the opposite of this, exacerbating the fear of terrorism by portraying it as an ever-present threat that requires extraordinary measures. But just as terrorism has been securitized through its framing as a threat unlike any other, it can be reframed and desecuritized, taken out of the realm of extraordinary measures and placed back into the realm of normal politics.

There are examples in the recent past of states that have successfully moved specific terrorist campaigns off the security agenda. In Turkey the calls for a Kurdish state had been interpreted as an existential threat to the Republic since 1961, and this intensified when the Kurdish Workers' Party (PKK) abandoned its ceasefire in 2004 and began again attacking Turkey. Despite this, from 2008 President Erdoğan and others in Turkey's government began desecuritizing the threat of Kurdish separatism. Initially this was aimed towards the Iraqi Kurdistan Regional Government (KRG) and took the form of high-level meetings between government officials, indicating a normalization of relations. Turkey began to refer to Iraqi Kurds in warm terms as relatives, brothers and neighbours, and economic relations were established, via access to the KRG's oil markets. During this time, the KRG was moved from the security agenda to the space of normal politics, and alongside this, Turkey's ruling Justice and Development Party initiated an opening with the PKK, with Erdoğan speaking about the need to solve the Kurdish issue through democratization and holding several high-level officials meeting with Abdullah Öcalan (the jailed PKK leader) which aimed to bring the insurgency to an end. At the same time, the backing of civil society and the media, along with the EU as an external backer, saw PKK terrorism and the Kurdish issue more broadly moved from the security agenda to the realm of normal politics. Much of this work has been undone since the outbreak of civil war in Syria and the destabilization of the region, and Turkey has again seen a resecuritization of Kurdish separatism, with the PKK becoming again classed as an existential threat requiring extraordinary measures to counter it. While this is ostensibly a failure to desecuritize terrorism in Turkey, it demonstrates that it *is* possible to remove a group or threat from the security agenda and deal with it using normal political means, where there is political and societal will to do so. It also shows that the ways states understand and conduct counterterrorism can change over time. Turkey's resecuritization of the Kurdish issue demonstrates only that to move from security to asecurity requires long-term thinking and political determination, and Turkey's recent collapse into increasingly authoritarian politics following the 2013 Gezi Protests and the coup attempt in 2016 is not conducive to the normalization of threats.

Other states have seen more long-term successes in the desecuritization of terrorism. After 9/11 the Colombian conflict with the Revolutionary Armed Forces of Colombia (FARC), ongoing since 1964, was subsumed under the macrosecuritization of the war on terror. Both the US and the Colombian government identified the battle with the FARC as key to the fight against terrorism, with Colombia's President Uribe arguing that there was no 'conflict', only attacks on democracy by terrorists. In 2010, when President Santos came to office, attempts were made to moderate the hard line rhetoric of his predecessor through what Sophie Haspeslagh has called a 'linguistic ceasefire', where the existence of a conflict was re-recognized and the terrorist label was abandoned, allowing the possibility for negotiations to take place between the government and militants, which eventually resulted in the peace deal ratified in November 2016.[2] Arguably a similar linguistic ceasefire took place during the Obama administration, when efforts were made to drop the rhetoric of the war of terror and move counterterrorism down the foreign policy agenda, positioning it as one threat among many for the US.[3] That US counterterrorism expanded quite significantly under Obama is testament to the limitations of reframing: desecuritization of terrorism is a necessary first step that opens up the possibility of finding solutions to terrorist violence, but if the problems of hybrid counterterrorism are to be solved, simply changing the representation of terrorism is not enough. Efforts need to be made to strengthen the normative and legal apparatuses eroded during the war on terror, in order to make way for more constructive approaches to countering it.

Reining in excessive powers

In the medium term there is a need to rein in excessive counterterrorism powers. Democracies' accruement of extraordinary powers to fight terrorism may be interpreted as a dangerous slide into authoritarianism. Such fears should not be dismissed, but we need not be too pessimistic. Legal, political and public pressure on governments can force states to reduce the scope of, or even abandon, egregious practices, and these approaches have met with some success. For example, in 2004 the UK House of Lords was instrumental in repealing provisions within the Anti-Terrorism Crime and Security Act (ATCSA) 2001 for the indefinite detention of foreign suspects (a derogation from the European Convention on Human Rights), arguing that detention was disproportionate, since the threat posed did not justify the removal of liberty, and discriminatory, since it was only used against foreign nationals. In this sense, the Law Lords did not question the securitization of the issue of terrorism but rather rejected the discriminatory and disproportionate powers used to deal with it. The push-back did force the government to remove discriminatory measures, however, it did so by extending the powers to all suspects (including British nationals) through control orders contained in the 2005 Prevention of Terrorism Act.[4]

In the early years of the war on terror, the US Supreme Court resisted indefinite detention in Guantánamo Bay in a similar way through legal opinions in *Rasul* v. *Bush* 2004, *Hamdan* v. *Rumsfeld* 2006 and *Boumediene* v. *Bush* 2007. These cases ruled that detainees could request federal courts to review the legality of their detention, established that the Geneva Conventions applied to military commissions in Guantánamo and confirmed that the US Constitution's fundamental rights extended to those held in overseas facilities.[5] The European Court of Human Rights (ECHR) has also been pivotal in addressing the excesses of counterterrorism measures, holding a number of states to account for their derogation from the European Convention on Human Rights (1953). Cases based on the ATCSA issue discussed earlier, *A. and Others* v. *the United Kingdom*, for example, were brought to the ECHR in 2009, which found the UK in violation of the right to have the lawfulness of a detention decided by a court. Other cases have concerned rendition, torture and detention, among others. For instance, two cases concerning the torture of individuals suspected of terrorism in Central Intelligence Agency (CIA) black sites in Poland (*Al Nashiri* v. *Poland* and *Husayn (Abu Zubaydah)* v. *Poland*) were upheld by the ECHR in 2014, which concluded that Poland had violated the convention's prohibition of torture (Article 3), along with the rights to: liberty and security (Article 5); respect for private and family life (Article 8); an effective remedy (Article 13); and a fair trial (Article 6 § 1).[6]

Cases have also been brought against security officials accused of torture or kidnapping. In 2008, Canadian federal courts demanded the release of interrogation videos at Guantánamo Bay of Canadian citizen Omar Khadr and instructed the government to seek his repatriation. Spanish, Italian, Swiss and German courts have also pursued prosecution of US officials involved in rendition and torture, including a successful Italian prosecution in November 2009 for the torture of Hassan Mustafa Osama Nasr (kidnapped from Milan and rendered to Egypt). In 2015 the ECHR confirmed its ruling that Poland had illegally permitted the CIA to operate a black site on its territory and ordered Poland to pay damages of US$250,000 to two plaintiffs who were tortured there. The assertion of the legal apparatus in these cases has held states and individuals responsible for their role in dubious counterterrorism practices and demonstrated that they cannot act with impunity.

The role of civil society in checking counterterrorism powers should also be noted. By holding accountable powerful interests, civil society and human rights groups have demonstrated that the legal apparatus can be used to ensure that excessive counterterrorist measures do not go unpunished. Under universal jurisdiction (which allows any state to investigate and prosecute people for serious international crimes), several investigations have been launched. For example, the Center for Constitutional Rights and the European Center for Constitutional Rights announced their intention to initiate criminal proceedings against George W. Bush in Switzerland ahead of a planned (and hastily cancelled) 2011 speaking engagement in Geneva, and Spanish courts filed cases in 2009 against the authors of the Torture Memos. In France a complaint was filed by human rights groups with the Paris prosecutor during a 2007 talk in the city by Donald Rumsfeld, who was charged with ordering and authorizing torture, and an investigation was launched in 2012 against former Guantánamo chief Geoffrey Miller regarding the treatment of three French citizens (Nizar Sassi, Mourad Benchellali and Khaled Ben Mustapha). Such cases have had limited success in the courts, due largely to the power of the US to reject extradition requests and grant immunity to US politicians for their actions in office. Nevertheless, these cases, along with the work of transnational activist and human rights groups such as Reprieve, the Rendition Project, INTERIGHTS, the Open Society Justice Initiative and the Helsinki Foundation for Human Rights, have helped to uncover and publicize the human rights violations of the war on terror, including European involvement in CIA rendition policies (linking Poland, Lithuania, Macedonia, Italy and Romania to these) which, as noted earlier, were successfully prosecuted in the ECHR.

In addition, politicians from within and outside governing parties have also engaged in democratic push-back against counterterrorism practices. The Dutch parliament, for example, consistently pressured the government to prevent those apprehended by Dutch forces in the Afghanistan War being turned over to the US, in order to ensure they were protected under the Geneva Conventions. Constructing their own bilateral agreement with the Afghan government and forging an agreement with Australians that captured fighters would be handed over to the Dutch, these practices were instituted to ensure that the Netherlands and Australia could not be implicated in US noncompliance with international law.[7]

While all these measures limited some of the pernicious effects of hybrid counterterrorism practices during the war on terror, they were clearly not enough to counter the damage done by such policies, and their existence can be fleeting. Bringing a court case against a state can take a considerable amount of time, especially to the ECHR, which often takes years. Checks and balances depend on the judicial activism of courts, in the form of their willingness to push back against egregious practices, which is likely to be more limited under illiberal governments. The key role played by civil society organizations, human rights groups and public pressure in all of these cases should still, however, leave room for optimism. The numerous humanitarian groups and think-tanks that have sprung up in states across the world to advocate for the rights of suspects and the repeal of excessive counterterrorism policies may offer hope, as well as the key role played by media and public pressure in holding states to account for human rights abuses and attacks on civil liberties. To prevent democracies sliding towards authoritarianism, it is vital that citizens be vigilant to attempts to push through extraordinary measures harmful to human rights in the name of counterterrorism.

Human security and non-violent counterterrorism

In the long term, a greater focus on human, rather than state, security is needed. If the practical goal of counterterrorism is to secure the individuals and society targeted, then at the most basic level this requires recognition of the humanity of all. Such approaches are often dismissed in the hard 'real' world of counterterrorism, which has historically favoured tough, violent approaches that project state power within and outside borders. But violent counterterrorism has not had many (if any) long-term successes and, as we've seen, it is often ineffective, inefficient or counterproductive. If terrorism makes those targeted want to hit back for the sake of revenge or justice, then why wouldn't the innocent victims of counterterrorism feel the same?

Approaching counterterrorism based on a recognition of the dignity and worth of human beings and an underlying commitment to reducing human suffering offers several advantages over the current way of doing things: it enables us to start where we are, without having to wait for utopias to arrive; it allows us to imagine better and more holistic approaches through an appreciation of the causes of terrorism and the role of counterterrorism in creating grievances; and it can help us to potentially realize better futures by minimizing and preventing suffering through a commitment to non-violent approaches to counterterrorism where possible.

Starting from where we are means that a counterterrorism committed to reducing human suffering does not depend on the arrival of a utopia. The tools for a counterterrorism that recognizes human dignity by the rule of law and human rights already exist, and they have the advantage of enjoying large-scale global public support and being already well established within the political cultures of specific states and global institutions. Liberal democracies have long-established constitutional principles of law and order that criminalize terrorism and provide a means to counter it via intelligence gathering, investigation, arrest and prosecution. These principles balance civil liberties with security, providing legislative and judicial oversight to hold the state constitutionally responsible for its actions, especially important given the covert nature of counterterrorism work. Peter Chalk argues that the three principles of limitation, credibility and accountability are crucial to keep in mind in the design of counterterrorism approaches. A limited and well-defined counterterrorism response ensures that actions do not go beyond what is required in the immediate situation; a credible response demonstrates that the state is acting in a necessary and effective way that protects civil liberties; and an accountable response ensures the state can be held responsible for its actions.[8] These principles have been eroded in many states, but as noted earlier, there is no reason why they cannot be reinvigorated. States that have employed dubious counterterrorism in the past have been able to reorient their campaigns, as did the British in Northern Ireland under the Major government, the Spanish government in its dealings with ETA and Colombia in its approach to the FARC.

In recent years, de-radicalization programmes have taken a central place in state efforts to counter terrorism, incorporating activities such as mentoring, counselling and theological discussion, which aim to end individuals' psychological commitment to a given ideology or cause. These potentially represent important non-violent tools to help individuals exit violent groups and contexts, however, the shaky theoretical foundations upon which they are based means that their effectiveness is far from clear. Based on the assumption that ideology is the key driver that moves individuals to choose violence as a means to resolve political grievances, de-radicalization programmes aim to convince them of the flaws of this way of thinking through theological debate, mentoring and counselling.[9] There is deep scholarly disagreement on the relative importance of ideology in individuals' decisions to engage in terrorist activities, but more pressingly for these programmes it is unclear what constitutes 'successful' de-radicalization and how this should be measured.[10] A more promising approach may be to concentrate on disengagement. While this frequently merges with de-radicalization, its focus is on behavioural, rather than ideological, change and it doesn't require individuals to renounce their convictions, just their use of violence. Research with those convicted of terrorism offences has shown that not all become involved for ideological reasons (with friendship and family ties acting as important non-ideological motivations for group membership) and that many who do engage in ideologically motivated terrorism may continue to hold 'radical' ideas even if they come to believe that violence is an ineffective or immoral way to achieve political change.[11] Targeting behavioural change thus offers a more theoretically sound basis for non-violent counterterrorism, and disengagement programmes which offer incentives to militants in return for abandoning violence have been effective in reducing terrorism and encouraging exit from militant groups in Italy, Spain, Northern Ireland

and Sweden. Resisting and rolling back militarized policing should also be a key area of focus, given the implications this has for those communities especially in the sights of counterterrorism forces. Restraints on the use of SWAT teams and an institutional move away from the 'warrior' mindset of paramilitary-style policing would help to restore the traditional role of police forces and avoid the counterproductive effects of counterterrorism policing. Ordinary policing has been effective in preventing terrorism because of the ability of officers to observe activism among radical groups, analyse criminal behaviour for links to terrorism and access information within communities.[12] Community policing, which aims to avoid the counterproductive effects of hard counterterrorism measures, has been shown to be effective in creating and maintaining the relationships within communities necessary for good cooperation and intelligence about terrorist activities. For example, the Youth and Police Initiative Plus programme in Boston brought together police and local Somali youth to develop greater understandings between those considered at risk of radicalization and local officers. The programme involved information-sharing by police as well as providing education and leadership development opportunities for Somalis, but it also specifically aimed to counter the lack of knowledge and understanding within the police force of local communities. Other community policing approaches have used similar methods, including the UK's Muslim Safety Forum, which was founded in 2001 to engage with the Metropolitan Police and MPs and to inform police policy. Through developing positive relations with Muslims in London and elsewhere, the Forum aimed to avoid the stigmatization and Othering of Muslims in the execution of counterterrorism policing. Although both of these initiatives were critiqued for their focus on Muslims, the use of soft power and community policing approaches were shown to be effective in de-escalating local tensions and encouraging community information-sharing.[13]

As noted in Chapter 1, widely shared and authoritative norms regarding human rights already exist in international humanitarian law (IHL) and the Just War principles enshrined in the Geneva Conventions of 1949 (which govern the treatment of armed forces personnel who fall into enemy hands, prohibiting torture, assaults on personal dignity and execution without trial) and the Additional Protocols I and II (1977), which restrain the behaviour of belligerents in international conflicts to protect civilians, prohibiting collective punishment and attacks on civilian hospitals and medical transports.

While the number of human rights violations that have taken place in conflict situations demonstrate that the effect of these norms have limitations, they nonetheless provide universally accepted rules for the conduct of international counterterrorism that clearly prohibit many of the problematic approaches discussed in this book: most obviously the torture and enhanced interrogation of terrorist suspects and targeted killing programmes. The previous chapter detailed how the impunity with which the US acted in holding suspects indefinitely and torturing them in Guantánamo Bay has enabled authoritarian governments to claim the same rights in their own treatment of terrorist suspects, as well as undermining international cooperation and the US's standing in the world. Trying or releasing the remaining detainees, in line with due process norms, and closing the detention centre down would restore some of this consistency and remove a key grievance against the US cited by terrorist groups across the world. Similarly, ending extensive targeted killing as a counterterrorism tool to restore the norm against assassination would realign states with the Conventions. This is not to suggest that such proposals are easy to put into practice: they are not, and they would face opposition from sections of the domestic population, just as violations of IHL do. Terrorism produces such visceral reactions because it targets non-combatants, denying them the basic right to life and liberty, and reducing them to a means to an end.[14] However, unlike terrorism, counterterrorism can always claim the moral high ground.

Respecting human rights as the foundation of counterterrorism is not just ethically sound; there is considerable evidence that it is effective as well. Walsh and Piazza studied 195 countries over several years and found that respect for physical integrity rights (those that protect individuals from extrajudicial murder, disappearance, torture or political imprisonment) substantially reduced terrorism. They argue that in democratic states adherence to the rule of law and human rights removes the opportunity for groups employing terrorism to accuse states of hypocrisy and brutality, lessens the chance that potential supporters will sympathize with the targeted group, and increases the likelihood of international sympathy and cooperation in countering the terrorism threat. Improving physical integrity rights from the lowest level by just one unit reduced the expected number of terrorist attacks by between 17 and 40 per cent, suggesting that countries with the poorest human rights records could see a large reduction in terrorism following even a very slight improvement in respect for human rights.[15] This suggests that the widely criticized programme of democracy promotion that marked the first years of the war on terror is not as important for terrorism reduction as promotion of human rights. And this is good news, as human rights have the significant advantage of enjoying near-universal support (all states have signed the Universal Declaration of Human Rights). At the same time, improving human rights involves fewer changes to the political and legal structures within states, and is considerably less costly to authoritarian regimes than democratic reforms. For democracies, respecting human rights ensures that terrorism is countered through means that are consistent with the democratic values of the society. Just as anti-democratic and anti-human rights norms have spread through the practice of the hybrid model, pro-democratic and pro-human rights norms can be spread through engaging in counterterrorism that respects these norms. At the same time, the humanization of the terrorist Other through this process also paves the way for conciliation and negotiation to bring a long-term end to terrorist campaigns.

There is no theoretical reason why non-violent approaches to counterterrorism cannot achieve the same tactical and strategic objectives that violent approaches do, at considerably lower human cost and with potentially fewer counterproductive effects.[16] In her book *How Terrorism Ends* Audrey Cronin studied the decline and demise of 457 groups using terrorism since 1968, and uncovered six pathways to ending terrorism campaigns: removal of the group's leader; entry of the group into legitimate political process; achievement of group's aims; implosion or loss of group's public support; group transition from terrorism into other forms of violence (such as criminal violence); and defeat and elimination by brute force.[17] Some of these transitions are not wholly within the control of counterterrorism forces, but the only approach that is entirely violent is the last one. For example, leadership removal in the 21st century has frequently been achieved through targeted killing, particularly by drone strike, of group leaders but there is no reason why this cannot be achieved through non-violent means. In both Peru and Turkey, the capture and jailing of leaders led to considerable reductions in violence and the decline of the movement after the apprehension of Shining Path's leader Abimael Guzmán by Peruvian police in 1992, and of PKK leader Abdullah Öcalan in 1999, both of whom called upon their respective constituencies to end violent attacks and the latter of which, as noted earlier, engaged in dialogue with the Turkish government to deal with broader grievances. Non-violent approaches are also available to counterterrorist forces in the form of strategies that encourage defections, disintegration or transformation. Peter Sederberg has noted several ways concessions may be used to degrade terrorist groups or reduce their violence.[18] Using concessions such as amnesties, for example, can encourage the abandonment of terrorism by exploiting divisions within a group to encourage the defection of moderate militants and diminish passive support of the movement. Offering plea deals in return for intelligence was successful in contributing to the disintegration of Italy's Red Brigades and ETA in Spain, and amnesties were central to peace processes in both Northern Ireland and Colombia.

Terrorism tempts states towards overreaction because the political objectives of a campaign are conflated with the violent tactics used, leading target states to the conclusion that the extreme tactics used mean that challenger groups must hold similarly extreme political objectives.[19] This works to encourage overreactions (as terrorist threats are viewed as existential) and discourage conciliation or negotiation. At the same time the possibility of understanding and dealing with groups' legitimate grievances is made more difficult. However, understanding these grievances, rather than waving them away if terrorist tactics are employed, opens up the possibility for negotiation and conciliation strategies to be considered as tools to achieve the same objectives as violent counterterrorism, at a lower human and material cost.

Civilians have a role to play here as agents who can employ non-violence effectively to counter terrorism by influencing armed groups to abide by norms of civilian protection. In FARC-controlled areas of Colombia, for example, civilians were successful in reducing violence by highlighting the inconsistencies between the behaviour of militants and their stated pro-peasant ideology. Through protests and talks, civilians demanded the institution of ethical norms in the treatment of non-combatants, and this resistance encouraged the surfacing of divisions within rebel groups about the legitimacy and usefulness of terrorism as a tactic to control civilians, which in turn caused fractures in the movement.[20] Similar resistances sought to reduce the violence of the Islamic State of Iraq and Syria (ISIS) as it took control of areas of Iraq and Syria in the mid-2010s. For example, teacher Suad Nofel engaged in regular silent protest walks to ISIS headquarters in Raqqa, carrying signs that challenged the Islamic legitimacy of militants' behaviour and demanded the release of kidnapped activists. Similarly, the human chain formed to protect Mosul's Crooked Mosque from destruction worked to undermine the legitimacy that ISIS claimed in these areas.[21] Other forms of resistance included attempts to disrupt the cooperation and obedience upon which the group depended. Through slow-downs and underperformance in administrative roles, civilians were able to undermine ISIS's claims to be able to provide services and act like a state. By targeting what the group valued and its claimed religious legitimacy, non-violent resistance aimed to persuade various audiences, including ISIS militants themselves, highlighting their actions as unjust, unfair and, most importantly, un-Islamic. ISIS was, of course, able to withstand public pressure because it chose brutal repression of the civilians that came under the group's control. But in doing so it undermined its own claimed legitimacy, failing to win the hearts and minds of the population and creating networks of non-violent resistance that exposed these abuses and generated moral outrage across the world.[22] States can learn from these examples by looking at what a group values and how it claims legitimacy. By targeting these in non-violent ways the moral high ground can be retained, and groups can be fractured as militants less convinced of the arguments justifying the use of violence peel away.

Historically, a number of leaders have stated unequivocally that negotiations with terrorists are off the table. The key argument for this stance is that to negotiate with actors who employ terrorism would legitimize this method, encourage others to use it to achieve their own demands, and demonstrate that terrorism is a viable strategy for political change. This assumes that groups using terrorism act rationally, according to cost–benefit calculations of the likely outcomes of specific tactics. But it also, implicitly, assumes that challenger groups have political objectives. As long as terrorism is understood as a means to a political end (rather than the entire identity of a group), there is no reason why conciliation strategies cannot be used as non-violent strategies designed to influence the behaviour of actors and draw them away from terrorism as a tactic. Conciliation strategies should not be understood as appeasement of terrorism, but as approaches that aim to bring the grievances that fuel it into the political sphere. Understanding that challenger groups are not monoliths means that factions favouring non-violent engagement can be targeted and strengthened in order to move groups to a path of transformation towards non-violent politics. As Harmonie Toros has argued, the British government under Prime Minister John Major moved towards accepting republicans in Northern Ireland as a legitimate group with legitimate grievances, which in turn helped to move the Provisional IRA and Sinn Fein towards a strategic shift. It was the opening of an alternative path to change that strengthened those factions favouring talks, encouraging the renunciation of violence and the movement's transformation towards becoming a legitimate entity.[23] As discussed earlier, similar openings were made by President Santos in Colombia towards the FARC. While such pathways are blocked, many groups will view violence as their only option.

Could al Qaeda be countered through non-violence?

Perhaps one of the most frequent arguments against non-violence as an approach to counterterrorism is raised in the case of groups with religious motivations, particularly al Qaeda and its offshoots. Critics argue that al Qaeda's goals and its violent methods demonstrate that for some challenger groups counter-violence is the only answer. The argument goes that groups like al Qaeda have totalistic goals to remake the world and an all-or-nothing approach that employs indiscriminately destructive methods. How could non-violent strategies be realistically used against them? And what possible role could conciliation or negotiation have in countering al Qaeda's terrorism?

The first thing to note in considering this argument is that extremely well-resourced violent counterterrorism has been turned against al Qaeda for the last quarter of a century. Operation Infinite Reach, in response to the 1998 al Qaeda-directed US embassy bombings in Kenya and Tanzania, launched cruise missiles on Sudan's Al-Shifa pharmaceutical plant along with al Qaeda training camps in Afghanistan's Khost Province, destroying the former and killing a number of militants in the latter case. However, rather than deterring terrorism, these attacks appear to have made bin Laden into a folk hero. After the 9/11 attacks, the US directed extraordinary resources to the violent countering of terrorism overseas. As noted earlier, President Bush stated in September 2001 that the war on terror would not end until every terrorist group of global reach had been defeated. As of March 2023, upwards of US$8 trillion has been spent on this exercise, engaging in counterterrorism activities, including air and drone strikes, ground combat operations, military exercises, and training and assistance of foreign forces, in more than 85 countries.[24] Two major ground wars have been conducted, in Afghanistan and Iraq, with air and/or drone strikes against militant groups in Pakistan, Afghanistan, Libya, Syria, Iraq, Somalia and Yemen. High-level leaders of al Qaeda and its affiliates have been killed, including the leaders of al Qaeda in Iraq (Abu Musab al-Zarqawi, killed in 2006) and al Qaeda in East Africa (Fazul Abdullah Mohammed, killed in 2011), as well as 'emirs' Osama bin Laden (2011) and Ayman al-Zawahiri (2022). Yet al Qaeda and its affiliates remain active in Afghanistan and Pakistan (AQ in the Indian Subcontinent), Yemen (AQ in the Arabian Peninsula) the Sahel and West Africa (Jama'a Nusrat ul-Islam wa al-Muslimin), Somalia and Kenya (al Shabaab) and North Africa (AQ in the Islamic Maghreb), not to mention ISIS offshoots in the Middle East, Central Asia, Central Africa, West Africa and South-East Asia. Clearly Bush's aims have not been achieved through violent counterterrorism.

The question remains then as to whether non-violent counterterrorism could do any better. In a horizontally organized group of 'leaderless jihad', with numerous offshoots across the world, there is no one leader to negotiate with. Who could negotiators talk to? Furthermore, what could be offered to such a group? How, realistically, could they be drawn into a political process and encouraged to abandon violence? While the proliferation of affiliate groups and the assassination of leaders bin Laden and al-Zawahiri means that talks with a single leader is not possible, the complexity of al Qaeda as a phenomenon potentially offers opportunities for deploying non-violent approaches to countering it.

Figures 5.1 and 5.2: Double-sided pictorial story leaflet produced by the US Department of Defense for air drops over Afghanistan during Operation Enduring Freedom (2001 or 2002)

The captions in Pashto and Arabic on recto (top image) read: 'Taliban do you think you are safe...?' and continue on verso (bottom image): 'in your tomb?'

The first step is to avoid presuming that all the affiliated groups discussed earlier have the same totalistic aims. As Toros has argued, in reality, local and regional groups allied to al Qaeda have local and regional objectives that frequently outweigh their broader commitments to the movement. Given the lack of hierarchical structure in al Qaeda, isolating particular elements is possible.

Toros gives the example of the Moro Islamic Liberation Front (MILF) in the Philippines, which maintained links with al Qaeda through financing and training in Pakistan and Afghanistan, but remained committed to its local goals: the creation of an autonomous region for the Moro people.[25] By resisting the temptation to view MILF as part of a clash of civilizations and avoiding classifying it as a terrorist organisation, the Philippines government was able to keep open the possibility of negotiations and in 2014 an historic peace agreement was reached, paving the way for the creation of a self-governing political entity, Bangsamoro. As of 2022 almost half of the group's 40,000 militants had been decommissioned and transitioned to civilian society through socioeconomic development programmes.

Audrey Cronin has argued that associations with al Qaeda may be little more than an evocative brand name that increases the profile and perceived strength of groups.[26] Rather than assuming that all affiliates hold to the same totalistic vision, analysis should be undertaken as to what these groups want and whether there exist legitimate grievances that might hold the possibility of negotiations. But what if, upon careful analysis, the goals of groups are found to be illegitimate? What if the goal is the establishment of a caliphate or the imposition of a non-representative government or system upon an unwilling group of people?

As noted earlier, the benefits of participating in terrorism can be reduced through non-violent deterrence, by manipulating the cost–benefit calculations of adversaries. For a religiously motivated group like al Qaeda, however, these calculations might be quite fundamentally skewed: for the spiritual rewards on offer, challenger groups may be willing to pay very high costs for the possibility of other-worldly rewards. Delegitimization is a key strategy in such cases and involves understanding what a group values and using its ideological rationale to influence behaviour. By attacking the legitimacy that is claimed for actions, the chance of a group achieving illegitimate or fringe goals may be reduced.

This requires attention to a group's narrative. Jerry Long and Alex Wilner argue that al Qaeda's narrative is used to conflate the current conflicts that Muslims face with ancient battles, to attract people to its cause, to legitimize the violence it uses, and to establish particular interpretations of current events.[27] This narrative can be understood as a weapon of war, which is directed at religious leaders and Muslims (with whom there is a battle to interpret Islam) and at the West (with whom there is a battle for the narrative of events), and it is this narrative that al Qaeda values the most, much more highly than it values fighters, training camps and other material assets. Because the narrative is what is most valued, it is at this level that deterrence would be most fruitful: 'Al-Qaida loses when its violent excesses are devoid of narratological meaning; when its behavior is deemed offensive and illegitimate by its audience; when its terrorism is judged as mere thuggery, intimidation, and baseless murder.'[28]

From this perspective, the war on terror has been counterproductive because it justified every aspect of al Qaeda's narrative, allowing it to be presented as a war against eternally besieged Muslims, justifying violence as a necessary and divinely sanctioned defence of the faith, and presenting events across the world as evidence of 'Jewish-Crusader' imperialism. Rather than feeding this narrative through violent counterterrorism, a more prudent response would emphasize the worldly concerns of local and national franchises to drive a doctrinal wedge between groups, treat militants as criminals rather than warriors, publicize the murder of Muslim civilians to highlight the disproportionate and illegitimate nature of jihadist violence, and support counternarratives that discredit al Qaeda's activities through Islamic ethics. By targeting what the group values – the narrative of religiously sanctioned violence – the group's legitimacy may be undermined with its target audiences. Exploiting this narrative is therefore key to weakening al Qaeda's credibility, by undermining the justification for violence that the group requires in order to remain legitimate in the eyes of its own constituency.

To realistically respond to terrorism, we have to recognize that it emerges out of specific sociopolitical contexts in which real grievances exist. Even while condemning terrorism as a tactic, we must accept that real structural and cultural violences underpin it and these need to be acknowledged and attended to if long-term solutions are going to succeed. This means that broad campaigns to end all forms of terrorism through violent repression are unlikely to be effective, simply because they do not tackle grievances and they usually create more.

What then would a better counterterrorism approach look like? A more effective and productive model would work on the basis of recognizing the humanity of all, including those who use terrorism and the communities and populations in which they reside. Labels such as 'terrorist', 'enemy combatant' and 'collateral damage' only corroborate claims by challenger groups that some lives are considered more worthy than others. To move forward, a more holistic counterterrorism should be undertaken with a view to reducing human suffering, based on a commitment to justice and a recognition that one's security cannot come at the expense of another's. In so doing, the means-ends thinking that has haunted hybrid counterterrorism could be avoided, through an approach that views human beings as ends in themselves and not just as means to an end.[29] Non-violent strategies can be used to achieve all the aims that have been pursued through violent counterterrorism, and conciliation and negotiation must be part of the counterterrorism toolbox. This means avoiding the temptation to declare groups that use terrorism as outside of the boundaries of dialogue. It also means appreciating the complex histories of violence that produce terrorism and a serious commitment to understanding the grievances that underpin these acts, including the role of counterterrorism in these dynamics.

6
CONCLUSION

O ur understanding of what counterterrorism is for rests on our definition of what terrorism is, and the infamous and long-standing struggle to define this means that counterterrorism has often occupied a grey area – understood in different ways according to the historical moment and the political persuasion of particular leaders and governments. Richard Jackson's definition of terrorism emphasizes the key reason why it is so morally repugnant: 'Terrorism is violence or its threat intended as a symbolically communicative act in which the direct victims of the action are instrumentalized as a means to creating a psychological effect of intimidation and fear in a target audience for a political objective.'[1]

Terrorism generates insecurity not just because of its random nature but because of its symbolic function. By instrumentalizing human beings and treating them as a means to a communicative end, terrorism violently projects the idea that victims have no moral worth in and of themselves. This is why these acts generate such outrage, and why the desire to hit back – to express the moral worth of the group targeted – is so strong. But through violent counterterrorism, the state signals the same message: that some humans have less moral worth than others. In responding to terrorism it is essential that states do not fall into this trap.

Counterterrorism, like terrorism, is a communicative act. Whether in the form of increased security measures at airports, 'see it, say it, sorted' posters in train and subway stations, protective concrete bollards in public squares, drone attacks on suspected leaders, preventative detention of suspects or pre-emptive military strikes against groups. All these acts, and the many more that comprise our contemporary security environment, make up the grammar of counterterrorism. They are themselves symbolic acts whose purpose is to send a message: reassuring a broader audience that the state is protecting them from harm. That many of these approaches involve instrumentalizing human beings of 'terrorist' appearance to send this message is the reason why counterterrorism has so often, in the past and the present, become indistinguishable from terrorism itself.

The focus on Islamist extremists as existential enemies has been useful for states, as fears of dangerous Others plotting against the national community encouraged public acquiescence to increasingly coercive counterterrorism powers. But this focus has meant that other terrorist threats, including those emerging from violent far-right, racist and misogynistic extremism, have received too little attention. These threats are currently rising up state agendas, but they are not at this point being constructed in existential terms. There is good reason to interpret this cynically. Minorities, marginalized groups and outside 'others' are usually the first to suffer when human rights norms are diminished in the name of counterterrorism, and clearly the resistance to framing such violence as existential is chiefly because it is largely committed by members of the dominant group (white men in the US and Europe, Hindu men in India, and so on), who cannot so easily be 'othered' and whose human rights are not so readily stripped away. Nevertheless, as the 2022 trials in the US demonstrate, it is in fact possible to address terrorism within the realm of normal politics, even when, as with the 6 January 2021 attack on the US Capitol, it actually does involve a plot to overthrow the government.

At the centre of all counterterrorism lies a question: what is more important, liberty or security? In the 21st century, the scales have tipped dramatically towards the latter, chiefly because terrorism has been so widely and consistently represented as a threat of existential proportions. But the accuracy of this claim is dubious to say the least. As is often noted in critical counterterrorism circles, in the global North you are statistically more likely to drown in your own bathtub than be a victim of terrorism,[2] and most nations that have enthusiastically embraced the war on terror have found themselves less, rather than more, secure.

The understanding that terrorism, like crime, is something that will not be eradicated, offers the chance for more realistic policy responses that frame counterterrorism as an allocation of scarce resources. As several scholars have argued, transparently representing the threat of terrorism can allow an informed public to engage in debate over the level of risk societies are willing to accept and the proportion of finite resources they are willing to dedicate to countering it. And it opens up space for an arguably more pertinent question about counterterrorism: security at what cost?

In autumn 2023, these debates were taking place worldwide after Hamas launched an unprecedented attack on Israeli civilians on 7 October, killing 1,200 and kidnapping more than 230 hostages. The Israeli government response to the attacks was depressingly familiar. Prime Minister Benjamin Netanyahu explicitly re-articulated the discourse of the war on terror in his 30 October statement to world media:

> Israel will stand against the forces of barbarism until victory. I hope and pray that civilized nations everywhere will back this fight. ... Israel's fight is your fight; because if Hamas and Iran's axis of evil win, you will be their next target. That's why Israel's victory will be your victory.[3]

Despite the attempts to draw the 'civilized' world into Israel's fight, the relentless bombardment of Gaza, the extraordinarily high death toll (estimated at more than 30,000 Palestinians killed within 145 days of the war, including at least 12,500 children), and the displacement of more than 1.2 million Gazans (75 per cent of the population) has led to outcry from humanitarian groups, civil society and the UN.[4]

The desire to hit back after attacks is all too human. But Israel has trodden the path of violent counterterrorism many times before and, as 7 October demonstrated, security from terrorism remains painfully elusive. As long as cycles of violence and retaliation continue, grievances will escalate and the possibility for the openings that lead to dialogue, conciliation and resolution are blocked. Prioritizing human rights and democratic norms and dealing sincerely with the very real grievances that underpin this conflict offer a more promising path to Israeli security in the long term. Such processes will not be easy, but ultimately the potential for positive change and genuine security lies in the recognition that any counterterrorism approach will be ineffective and counterproductive if it terrorizes other human beings in its efforts to secure the state.

Peter Sederberg argued in the mid-1990s that there had been a tendency to overinflate the effectiveness of repressive counterterrorism measures and underestimate the possibility that democratic principles such as negotiation, compromise and conciliation might themselves offer effective responses to terrorism.[5] In the 21st century, this is even more the case. Yet we stand at an important historical juncture, when the limitations and problems of violent counterterrorism are clearer than they have ever been. This creates the appetite and the opportunity for thinking through different solutions. By demanding that human, rather than state, security be prioritized, energy can be directed towards imagining, instituting and realizing better futures in our efforts to counter the violence of both terrorism and counterterrorism.

NOTES

Chapter 1

1   Alex Peter Schmid, 'Revisiting the Wicked Problem of Defining Terrorism', *Contemporary Voices* 1, no. 4 (2020): pp 3–11.

2   Max Weber, 'Politics as a Vocation', in *From Max Weber: Essays in Sociology*, ed H.H. Gerth and C. Wright Mills (Routledge, 2009), p 78.

3   George W. Bush, 'Address to a Joint Session of Congress and the American People', Whitehouse Archives, 20 September 2001, https://georgewbush-whitehouse.archives.gov/news/releases/2001/09/20010920-8.html.

4   John Mueller and Mark G. Stewart, 'Terrorism and Bathtubs: Comparing and Assessing the Risks', *Terrorism and Political Violence* 33, no. 1 (2021): p 139.

5   Alex Peter Schmid, 'Defining Terrorism' (International Centre for Counter-Terrorism, March 2023), https://www.icct.nl/sites/default/files/2023-03/Schmidt%20-%20Defining%20Terrorism_1.pdf.

6   Federal Bureau of Investigation, 'Terrorism', Folder, Federal Bureau of Investigation, https://www.fbi.gov/investigate/terrorism.

7   Bureau of Counterterrorism, 'Country Reports on Terrorism 2021' (US Department of State, 2022), https://www.state.gov/reports/country-reports-on-terrorism-2021/.

8   Nicholas J. Perry, 'The Numerous Federal Legal Definitions of Terrorism: The Problem of Too Many Grails', *Journal of Legislation* 30 (2003): pp 249–74.

9   Mary S. Barton, 'The Global War on Anarchism: The United States and International Anarchist Terrorism, 1898–1904', *Diplomatic History* 39, no. 2 (2015): p 315.

10 Harry W. Shlaudeman, 'The "Third World War" and South America', ARA Monthly Report (July) (Washington, DC: Department of State, 3 August 1976), https://nsarchive2.gwu.edu/NSAEBB/NSAEBB125/condor05.pdf.

11   Ronald Reagan, 'Remarks at the Annual Convention of the American Bar Association', 8 July 1985, https://www.presidency.ucsb.edu/documents/remarks-the-annual-convention-the-american-bar-association.

12   Elena Dück and Robin Lucke, 'Same Old (Macro-) Securitization? A Comparison of Political Reactions to Major Terrorist Attacks in the United States and France', *Croatian International Relations Review* 25, no. 84 (2019): p 10.

13   Sidney Aster, 'Appeasement: Before and After Revisionism', *Diplomacy and Statecraft* 19, no. 3 (2008): pp 443–80.

14   Barry Buzan and Ole Wæver, 'Macrosecuritization and Security Constellations: Reconsidering Scale in Securitization Theory', *Review of International Studies* 35, no. 2 (2009): pp 253–76.

Chapter 2

1   Ronald Crelinsten, *Counterterrorism* (Polity Press, 2009).

2   George M. Clifford, 'Just Counterterrorism', *Critical Studies on Terrorism* 10, no. 1 (2017): p 75.

3   Leonard Weinberg, 'The Red Brigades', in *Democracy and Counterterrorism: Lessons from the Past*, ed Robert J. Art and Louise Richardson (United States Institute of Peace, 2007), pp 25–62.

4   Crelinsten, *Counterterrorism*, p 59.

5   Human Rights Watch, 'India: No Justice for 1984 Anti-Sikh Bloodshed', 29 October 2014, https://www.hrw.org/news/2014/10/29/india-no-justice-1984-anti-sikh-bloodshed.

6   Jennifer Giroux and Michael Nwankpa, 'A Vicious Cycle: The Growth of Terrorism and Counterterrorism in Nigeria, 1999–2016', in *Non-Western Responses to Terrorism*, ed Michael J Boyle (Manchester University Press, 2019), p 686.

7   Human Rights Watch, 'If You Are Afraid for Your Lives, Leave Sinai!', *Human Rights Watch*, 28 May 2019, https://www.hrw.org/report/2019/05/28/if-you-are-afraid-your-lives-leave-sinai/egyptian-security-forces-and-isis.

8   Alex Wilner, 'Fencing in Warfare: Threats, Punishment, and Intra-War Deterrence in Counterterrorism', *Security Studies* 22, no. 4 (2013): p 742.

9   Crelinsten, *Counterterrorism*, p 12.

10   United Nations, 'Charter of the United Nations', United Nations (United Nations, 24 October 1945), https://www.un.org/en/about-us/un-charter/full-text.

11   Abraham D. Sofaer, 'On the Necessity of Pre-emption', *European Journal of International Law* 14, no. 2 (2003): p 219.

12   The President of the United States, 'The National Security Strategy of the United States of America' (Washington, DC: State Department, 17 September 2002), 19, https://2009-2017.state.gov/documents/organization/63562.pdf.

13   Alex J. Bellamy, 'Pre-Empting Terror', in *Security and the War on Terror*, ed Alex J. Bellamy, Roland Bleiker, Sara E. Davies, Richard Devetak (Routledge, 2007), p 118.

14   Michael Schmitt, 'State-Sponsored Assassination in International and Domestic Law', *Yale Journal of International Law* 17 (1992): pp 609–85.

15   David Kretzmer, 'Targeted Killing of Suspected Terrorists: Extra-Judicial Executions or Legitimate Means of Defence?', *European Journal of International Law* 16, no. 2 (2005): pp 171–212.

16   Giroux and Nwankpa, 'A Vicious Cycle', p 670.

17   Christopher Kutz, 'How Norms Die: Torture and Assassination in American Security Policy', *Ethics & International Affairs* 28, no. 4 (2014): pp 425–49.

18   Bush, 'Address to a Joint Session of Congress and the American People'.

19   International Committee of the Red Cross, 'Convention (IV) Relative to the Protection of Civilian Persons in Time of War. Geneva, 12 August 1949. Commentary of 1958', 1958, https://ihl-databases.icrc.org/en/ihl-treaties/gciv-1949/article-4/commentary/1958.

20   Amnesty International, 'Guantánamo Bay: Over 20 Years of Injustice', August 2023, https://www.amnesty.org.uk/guantanamo-bay-human-rights.

21   Lex Lasry, QC, 'Military Justice: David Hicks and Guantanamo Bay', in *Counter-Terrorism and the Post-Democratic State*, ed Jenny Hocking and Colleen Lewis (Edward Elgar Publishing, 2007), pp 48–56.

22   UN General Assembly, 'Convention against Torture and Other Cruel, Inhuman or Degrading Treatment or Punishment. United Nations, Treaty Series', 1465 § (1984), art. 1, https://treaties.un.org/doc/Publication/UNTS/Volume%201465/volume-1465-I-24841-English.pdf.

23   Jay Bybee, 'Memorandum for Alberto R. Gonzales Counsel to the President Re: Standards of Conduct for Interrogation under 18 USC §§2340–2340A', *The Rendition Project*, 1 August 2002,

13, https://www.therenditionproject.org.uk/pdf/PDF%2019%20 [Bybee%20Memo%20to%20Gonzales%20Standards%20 Interrogation%201%20Aug.pdf.

24 Rebecca Sanders, 'Human Rights and Counterterrorism: The American "Global War on Terror"', in *Human Rights in War*, ed Damien Rogers, International Human Rights (Springer Nature Singapore, 2022), p 429.

25 Senate Select Committee on Intelligence, 'The Central Intelligence Agency's Detention and Interrogation Program' (Washington, DC: United States Senate, 9 December 2014), vi, https://www. intelligence.senate.gov/sites/default/files/publications/CRPT-113srpt288.pdf.

26 Jeremy Prestholdt, 'Counterterrorism in Kenya: Security Aid, Impunity and Muslim Alienation', in *Non-Western Responses to Terrorism*, ed Michael J Boyle (Manchester University Press, 2019), pp 618–19.

27 David Carpenter, 'Magna Carta 1215: Its Social and Political Context', in *Magna Carta: History, Context and Influence*, ed Lawrence Goldman (University of London Press, 2018), p 20.

28 Tiberiu Dragu, 'Is There a Trade-off between Security and Liberty? Executive Bias, Privacy Protections, and Terrorism Prevention', *The American Political Science Review* 105, no. 1 (2011): p 66.

29 Jenny Hocking and Colleen Lewis, 'Counter-Terrorism and the Rise of "Security Policing"', in *Counter-Terrorism and the Post-Democratic State*, ed Jenny Hocking and Colleen Lewis (Edward Elgar Publishing, 2007), p 139.

30 Lucia Zedner, 'Securing Liberty in the Face of Terror: Reflections from Criminal Justice', *Journal of Law and Society* 32, no. 4 (2005): p 524.

31 Andrew Lynch, Nicola McGarrity and George Williams, 'The Emergence of a "Culture of Control"', in *Counter-Terrorism and Beyond: The Culture of Law and Justice After 9/11*, ed Andrew Lynch, Nicola McGarrity and George Williams (Taylor & Francis, 2010), p 5.

32 Stefanie Kam and Michael Clarke, 'Securitization, Surveillance and "De-extremization" in Xinjiang', *International Affairs* 97, no. 3 (2021): pp 625–42.

33 Roel Meijer, 'Islam and Saudi Arabia's Counterterrorism Strategy', in *Non-Western Responses to Terrorism*, ed Michael J. Boyle (Manchester University Press, 2019), pp 545–52.

34 Jon Ungoed-Thomas and Mark Townsend, 'Revealed: Plan to Brand Anyone "Undermining" UK as Extremist', *Observer*, 4 November 2023, https://www.theguardian.com/uk-news/2023/nov/04/plans-to-redefine-extremism-would-include-undermining-uk-values.

35 Kam and Clarke, 'Securitization, Surveillance and "De-extremization" in Xinjiang', p 625.

36 Mary Manjikian, 'Walking a Thin Line: The Netherland's Counterterrorism Challenge', in *The Palgrave Handbook of Global Counterterrorism Policy*, ed Scott N. Romaniuk, Francis Grice, Daniela Irrera and Stewart Webb (Palgrave, 2017), pp 385–6.

Chapter 3

1 Dick Cheney, 'The Vice President Appears on Meet the Press with Tim Russert', George W Bush Whitehouse Archives, 15 September 2001, https://georgewbush-whitehouse.archives.gov/vicepresident/news-speeches/speeches/vp20010916.html.

2 Bush, 'Address to a Joint Session of Congress and the American People'.

3 Condoleezza Rice, 'Dr. Condoleezza Rice Discusses President's National Security Strategy', George W. Bush Whitehouse Archives, 1 October 2002, https://georgewbush-whitehouse.archives.gov/news/releases/2002/10/print/20021001-6.html.

4 Francis Fukuyama, 'The End of History?', *The National Interest*, no. 16 (1989): p 3.

5 John Fousek, *To Lead the Free World: American Nationalism and the Cultural Roots of the Cold War* (University of North Carolina Press, 2000).

6 The President of the United States, 'The National Security Strategy of the United States of America'.

7 S.P. Huntington, 'The Clash of Civilizations?', *Foreign Affairs* 72, no. 3 (1993): p 35.

8 Bush, 'Address to a Joint Session of Congress and the American People'.

9 Ervand Abrahamian, 'The US Media, Huntington and September 11', *Third World Quarterly* 24, no. 3 (2003): pp 529–44.

10 George W. Bush, 'President Bush Speaks to United Nations', 10 November 2001, https://georgewbush-whitehouse.archives.gov/news/releases/2001/11/20011110-3.html.

11   David C. Rapoport, *Waves of Global Terrorism: From 1879 to the Present* (Columbia University Press, 2022).

12   Richard Jensen, 'Daggers, Rifles and Dynamite: Anarchist Terrorism in Nineteenth Century Europe', *Terrorism and Political Violence* 16, no. 1 (2004): pp 116–53.

13   Theodore Roosevelt, 'First Annual Message to the Senate and House of Representatives', The American Presidency Project, 3 December 1901, https://www.presidency.ucsb.edu/documents/first-annual-message-16.

14   Matthew Carr, *The Infernal Machine: A History of Terrorism from the Assassination of Tsar Alexander II to al-Qaeda* (The New Press, 2006), p 41.

15   John M. Merriman, *The Dynamite Club: How a Bombing in Fin-De-Siècle Paris Ignited the Age of Modern Terror* (Yale University Press, 2016), pp 207–8.

16   Beatrice de Graaf, 'The Black International Conspiracy as Security Dispositive in the Netherlands, 1880–1900', *Historical Social Research/Historische Sozialforschung* 38, no. 1 (143) (2013): p 148.

17   Richard Jensen, 'The Pre-1914 Anarchist "Lone Wolf" Terrorist and Governmental Responses', *Terrorism and Political Violence* 26 (2014): p 88.

18   Barton, 'The Global War on Anarchism', p 310.

19   Michael E. Newell, 'How the Normative Resistance of Anarchism Shaped the State Monopoly on Violence', *European Journal of International Relations* 25, no. 4 (2019): p 1249.

20   Jeffrey Monaghan, 'Settler Governmentality and Racializing Surveillance in Canada's North-West', *The Canadian Journal of Sociology/Cahiers Canadiens de Sociologie* 38, no. 4 (2013): pp 487–508.

21   Radhika Singha, 'Settle, Mobilize, Verify: Identification Practices in Colonial India', *Studies in History* 16, no. 2 (2000): p 191.

22   Christopher Paul, Colin P. Clarke, Beth Grill and Molly Dunigan, *Paths to Victory: Detailed Insurgency Case Studies* (RAND Corporation, 2013), p 75.

23   John McCracken, 'In the Shadow of Mau Mau: Detainees and Detention Camps during Nyasaland's State of Emergency', *Journal of Southern African Studies* 37, no. 3 (2011): p 537.

24   David French, *The British Way in Counter-Insurgency, 1945–1967* (Oxford University Press, 2011), pp 160–1.

25   Marnia Lazreg, 'Algeria as Template: Torture and Counter-Insurgency War', *Global Dialogue* 12, no. 1 (2010): p 3.

26   Wolfgang Form, 'Charging Waterboarding as a War Crime: U.S. War Crime Trials in the Far East after World War II', *Chapman Journal of Criminal Justice* 2, no. 1 (2011): pp 253–4.

27   Daniel Branch, 'Footprints in the Sand: British Colonial Counterinsurgency and the War in Iraq', *Politics & Society* 38, no. 1 (2010): pp 18–20.

28   Lisa Stampnitzky, *Disciplining Terror: How Experts Invented 'Terrorism'* (Cambridge University Press, 2013), p 21.

29   Martin J. McCleery, *Operation Demetrius and Its Aftermath: A New History of the Use of Internment Without Trial in Northern Ireland 1971–75* (Manchester University Press, 2015), p 33.

30   Rashid I. Khalidi, 'From the Editor: Israel: A Carceral State', *Journal of Palestine Studies* 43, no. 4 (2014): pp 5–6.

31   Gershon Shafir, 'Torturing Democracies: The Curious Debate over the "Israeli Model"', in *National Insecurity and Human Rights: Democracies Debate Counterterrorism*, ed Alison Brysk and Gershon Shafir (University of California Press, 2007), pp 96–8.

32   Michael P. O'Connor and Celia M. Rumann, 'Into the Fire: How to Avoid Getting Burned by the Same Mistakes Made Fighting Terrorism in Northern Ireland', *Cardazo Law Review* 24, no. 4 (2003): p 1690.

33   Ernest Evans, 'Goodness Armed with Power: Lessons from Other Democracies for the U.S. War on Terrorism', *World Affairs* 166, no. 3 (2004): p 130.

34   Jorge E. Delgado, 'The Colombian Case: Rebranding Counterinsurgency as Counterterrorism', in *The Palgrave Handbook of Global Counterterrorism Policy*, ed Scott N. Romaniuk, Francis Grice, Daniela Irrera and Stewart Webb (Palgrave, 2017), p 298.

35   José Pedro Zúquete, 'Counterterrorism in Brazil: From Dictatorship to Democratic Times', in *The Palgrave Handbook of Global Counterterrorism Policy*, ed Scott N. Romaniuk, Francis Grice, Daniela Irrera and Stewart Webb (Palgrave, 2017), p 278.

36   Marguerite Feitlowitz, 'Night and Fog in Argentina', *Salmagundi*, no. 94/95 (1992): p 41.

37   Daniel Byman, *A High Price: The Triumphs and Failures of Israeli Counterterrorism* (Oxford University Press, 2011), pp 52–3.

38 Peter Chalk, 'The Response to Terrorism as a Threat to Liberal Democracy', *Australian Journal of Politics and History* 44, no. 3 (1998): pp 377–9.

39 Omar G. Encarnación, 'Democracy and Dirty Wars in Spain', *Human Rights Quarterly* 29, no. 4 (2007): p 954.

40 Salvador Martí, Pilar Domingo, and Ibarra Pedro, 'Democracy, Civil Liberties, and Counterterrorist Measures in Spain', in *National Insecurity and Human Rights: Democracies Debate Counterterrorism*, ed Alison Brysk and Gershon Shafi (University of California Press, 2007), p 129.

41 Vincent Bevins, *The Jakarta Method: Washington's Anticommunist Crusade and the Mass Murder Program That Shaped Our World* (Public Affairs, 2020).

42 Ian Hurd, *How to Do Things with International Law* (Princeton University Press, 2017).

Chapter 4

1 Costs of War Project, 'U.S. Budgetary Costs of Post-9/11 Wars Through FY2022: $8 Trillion' (Brown University: Watson Institute of International and Public Affairs, 1 September 2021), https://watson.brown.edu/costsofwar/figures/2021/BudgetaryCosts.

2 Stimson Study Group, 'Counterterrorism Spending: Protecting America While Promoting Efficiencies and Accountability' (Stimson Center, 2018), 20, https://www.stimson.org/wp-content/files/file-attachments/CT_Spending_Report_0.pdf.

3 Beatrice De Graaf and Bob De Graaff, 'Bringing Politics Back in: The Introduction of the "Performative Power" of Counterterrorism', *Critical Studies on Terrorism* 3, no. 2 (2010): p 264.

4 C.W. Haerpfer, R. Inglehart, A. Moreno, C. Welzel, K. Kizilova, J. Diez-Medrano, M. Lagos, P. Norris, E. Ponarin & B. Puranen, 'World Values Survey: Round Seven – Country-Pooled Datafile' (JD Systems Institute & WVSA Secretariat, 2022), https://doi.org/10.14281/18241.1; START (National Consortium for the Study of Terrorism and Responses to Terrorism), 'Global Terrorism Database 1970–2020 [Zimbabwe Data File]', 2022, https://www.start.umd.edu/gtd.

5 Gallup, 'In Depth: Terrorism', Gallup.com, 2023, https://news.gallup.com/poll/4909/Terrorism-United-States.aspx.

6 De Graaf and De Graaff, 'Bringing Politics Back In', p 265.

7   T.W. van Dongen, 'Break It Down: An Alternative Approach to Measuring Effectiveness in Counterterrorism', *Journal of Applied Security Research* 6, no. 3 (2011): pp 357–71.

8   John Morrison, 'Reality Check: The Real IRA's Tactical Adaptation and Restraint in the Aftermath of the Omagh Bombing', *Perspectives on Terrorism* 14, no. 6 (2020): pp 152–64.

9   McCleery, *Operation Demetrius and Its Aftermath*.

10 Eric Van Um and Daniela Pisoiu, 'Dealing with Uncertainty: The Illusion of Knowledge in the Study of Counterterrorism Effectiveness', *Critical Studies on Terrorism* 8, no. 2 (2015): pp 229–45.

11 Charles F. Parker, Eric K. Stern, Eric Paglia and Christer Brown, 'Preventable Catastrophe? The Hurricane Katrina Disaster Revisited', *Journal of Contingencies and Crisis Management* 17, no. 4 (2009): p 215.

12 Mueller and Stewart, 'Terrorism and Bathtubs', p 142.

13 The Guardian, 'Judge Rules 9/11 Defendant Unfit for Trial after CIA Torture Made Him Psychotic', 22 September 2023, https://www.theguardian.com/us-news/2023/sep/22/september-11-defendant-declared-unfit-trial-cia-abuse-psychotic.

14 Sacha Pfeiffer, 'A Legacy of Torture Is Preventing Trials at Guantánamo', *NPR*, 14 November 2019, https://www.npr.org/2019/11/14/778944195/a-legacy-of-torture-is-preventing-trials-at-guant-namo.

15 Andrew Silke, 'Fire of Iolaus: The Role of State Countermeasures in Causing Terrorism and What Needs to Be Done', in *Root Causes of Terrorism: Myths, Reality and Ways Forward*, ed Tore Bjørgo (Routledge, 2005), p 241.

16 Stephanie Savell, 'The Costs of United States' Post-9/11 "Security Assistance": How Counterterrorism Intensified Conflict in Burkina Faso and Around the World', 20 Years of War: A Costs of War Research Series (Brown University: Watson Institute of International and Public Affairs, 4 March 2021), https://watson.brown.edu/costsofwar/files/cow/imce/papers/2021/Costs%20of%20Counterterrorism%20in%20Burkina%20Faso_Costs%20of%20War_Savell.pdf.

17 Nick Turse, 'Another U.S.-Trained Soldier Stages a Coup in West Africa', *The Intercept*, 26 January 2022, https://theintercept.com/2022/01/26/burkina-faso-coup-us-military/.

18 United Nations Development Programme, *Journey to Extremism in Africa: Pathways to Recruitment and Disengagement* (United Nations, 2023), 90, https://doi.org/10.18356/9789210025812.

19 Michael J. Boyle, 'The Costs and Consequences of Drone Warfare', *International Affairs* 89, no. 1 (2013): p 11.

20 Bryce Loidolt, 'Were Drone Strikes Effective? Evaluating the Drone Campaign in Pakistan Through Captured al-Qaeda Documents', *Texas National Security Review* 5, no. 2 (2022): p 78.

21 Boyle, 'The Costs and Consequences of Drone Warfare'.

22 International Human Rights and Conflict Resolution Clinic (Stanford Law School) and Global Justice Clinic (NYU School of Law), 'Living Under Drones: Death, Injury, and Trauma to Civilians from US Drone Practices in Pakistan', September 2012, https://doi.org/10.1163/2468-1733_shafr_SIM260090013.

23 Chalk, 'The Response to Terrorism as a Threat to Liberal Democracy', p 375.

24 Chalk, 'The Response to Terrorism as a Threat to Liberal Democracy', p 386.

25 Jessica Wolfendale, 'Terrorism, Security, and the Threat of Counterterrorism', *Studies in Conflict & Terrorism* 30, no. 1 (2007): p 88.

26 Antony Field, 'The Dynamics of Terrorism and Counterterrorism: Understanding the Domestic Security Dilemma', *Studies in Conflict & Terrorism* 40, no. 6 (2017): p 471.

27 Ismail Onat and Serdar San, 'Global Displacement of ISIS Activities and the Effectiveness of Police Arrests as a Means of Deterrence', in *From Territorial Defeat to Global ISIS: Lessons Learned*, ed Jack A. Goldstone, Eitan Y. Alimi, Suleyman Ozeren and Suat Cubukcu (IOS Press, 2021), p 188.

28 Suzanne Ito, 'American Citizen Anwar Al-Aulaqi Killed Without Judicial Process', *American Civil Liberties Union*, 30 September 2011, https://www.aclu.org/news/national-security/aclu-lens-american-citizen-anwar-al-aulaqi-killed-without.

29 Igor Primoratz, 'State Terrorism', in *Terrorism and Justice: Moral Argument in a Threatened World*, ed Tony Coady and Michael O'Keefe (Melbourne University Publishing, 2002), pp 37–8.

30 Rashmi Singh, 'Counterterrorism in India: An Ad Hoc Response to an Enduring and Variable Threat', in *Non-Western Responses to Terrorism*, ed Michael J. Boyle (Manchester University Press, 2019), pp 283–4.

[31] Martha Finnemore and Kathryn Sikkink, 'International Norm Dynamics and Political Change', *International Organization* 52, no. 4 (1998): p 892.

[32] Laurie R. Blank, 'The Consequences of a War Paradigms for Counterterrorism: What Impact on Basic Rights and Values', *Georgia Law Review* 46, no. 3 (2012): p 733.

[33] Averell Schmidt and Kathryn Sikkink, 'Breaking the Ban? The Heterogeneous Impact of US Contestation of the Torture Norm', *Journal of Global Security Studies* 4, no. 1 (2019): p 111.

[34] Boyle, 'The Costs and Consequences of Drone Warfare', p 28.

[35] David Keen, 'War without End? Magic, Propaganda and the Hidden Functions of Counter-Terror', *Journal of International Development* 18, no. 1 (2006): p 90.

Chapter 5

[1] John Mueller, 'Terrorism and the Dynamics of Threat Exaggeration', in *Prepared for Presentation at the 2005 Annual Meeting of the American Political Science Association, Washington, DC, September 1–4, 2005* (Washington, DC, 2005), p 39.

[2] Sophie Haspeslagh, 'The "Linguistic Ceasefire": Negotiating in an Age of Proscription', *Security Dialogue* 52, no. 4 (2021): pp 361–79.

[3] Trevor McCrisken, 'Ten Years on: Obama's War on Terrorism in Rhetoric and Practice', *International Affairs* 87, no. 4 (2011): pp 781–801.

[4] Jonathan Bright, 'Securitization, Terror, and Control: Towards a Theory of the Breaking Point', *Review of International Studies* 38, no. 4 (2012): pp 861–79.

[5] Jules Lobel, 'Victory without Success: The Guantanamo Litigation, Permanent Preventative Detention and Resisting Injustice', *Journal of Law in Society* 14, no. 1 (2013): pp 121–66.

[6] European Court of Human Rights, 'Terrorism and the European Convention on Human Rights', February 2024, https://www.echr.coe.int/documents/d/echr/fs_terrorism_eng.

[7] Schmidt and Sikkink, 'Breaking the Ban?', p 112.

[8] Chalk, 'The Response to Terrorism as a Threat to Liberal Democracy', pp 386–7.

[9] John Horgan and Kurt Braddock, 'Rehabilitating the Terrorists? Challenges in Assessing the Effectiveness of De-radicalization

Programs', *Terrorism and Political Violence* 22, no. 2 (2010):
pp 267–91.

[10] Daniel Koehler, 'How and Why We Should Take Deradicalization Seriously', *Nature Human Behaviour* 1, no. 6 (May 2017): p 1.

[11] Timothy Williams, 'Ideological and Behavioural Radicalisation into Terrorism – an Alternative Sequencing', *Journal for Deradicalization* Summer, no. 19 (2019): pp 85–121.

[12] David H. Bayley and David Weisburd, 'Cops and Spooks: The Role of Police in Counterterrorism', in *To Protect and To Serve: Policing in an Age of Terrorism*, ed David Weisburd, Thomas E. Feucht, Idit Hakimi, Lois Felson Mock and Simon Perry (Springer Verlag, 2009), pp 81–99.

[13] Martin Innes, 'Policing Uncertainty: Countering Terror through Community Intelligence and Democratic Policing', *Annals of The American Academy of Political and Social Science* 605, no. 1 (2006): pp 222–41.

[14] Clifford, 'Just Counterterrorism', p 68.

[15] James I. Walsh and James A. Piazza, 'Why Respecting Physical Integrity Rights Reduces Terrorism', *Comparative Political Studies* 43, no. 5 (2010): p 566.

[16] Richard Jackson, 'CTS, Counterterrorism and Non-Violence', *Critical Studies on Terrorism* 10, no. 2 (2017): pp 357–69.

[17] Audrey Kurth Cronin, *How Terrorism Ends: Understanding the Decline and Demise of Terrorist Campaigns* (Princeton University Press, 2009), p 25.

[18] Peter C. Sederberg, 'Conciliation as Counter-Terrorist Strategy', *Journal of Peace Research* 32, no. 3 (1995): p 307.

[19] Max Abrahms, 'The Political Effectiveness of Terrorism Revisited', *Comparative Political Studies* 45, no. 3 (2012): p 383.

[20] Oliver Kaplan, 'Nudging Armed Groups: How Civilians Transmit Norms of Protection', *Stability: International Journal of Security & Development* 2, no. 3 (2013): pp 9–10.

[21] Maria J. Stephan, 'Civil Resistance vs ISIS', *Journal of Resistance Studies* 1, no. 2 (2015): p 136. The mosque was eventually destroyed by ISIS during the battle of Mosul in 2017.

[22] Roberto Baldoli, 'Fighting Terrorism with Nonviolence: An Ideological Perspective', *Critical Studies on Terrorism* 13, no. 3 (2020): p 467.

[23] Harmonie Toros, '"We Don't Negotiate with Terrorists!": Legitimacy and Complexity in Terrorist Conflicts', *Security Dialogue* 39, no. 4 (2008): p 416.

24   Costs of War Project, 'The Costs of War', The Costs of War, March
      2023, https://watson.brown.edu/costsofwar/home.
25   Toros, '"We Don't Negotiate with Terrorists!"', p 420.
26   Cronin, *How Terrorism Ends*.
27   Jerry Mark Long and Alex S. Wilner, 'Delegitimizing Al-Qaida:
      Defeating an "Army Whose Men Love Death"', *International
      Security* 39, no. 1 (2014): pp 130–1.
28   Long and Wilner, 'Delegitimizing Al-Qaida', p 150.
29   Sondre Lindahl, 'A CTS Model of Counterterrorism', *Critical
      Studies on Terrorism* 10, no. 3 (2017): pp 523–41.

Chapter 6

1   Richard Jackson, 'In Defence of "Terrorism": Finding a Way
     through a Forest of Misconceptions', *Behavioral Sciences of
     Terrorism and Political Aggression* 3, no. 2 (2011): p 123.
2   Mueller and Stewart, 'Terrorism and Bathtubs'.
3   Amy Spiro, 'Netanyahu Tells Foreign Press: Calls for a Ceasefire
     Are Calls for Israel to Surrender', *The Times of Israel*, 30 October
     2023, https://www.timesofisrael.com/liveblog_entry/netanyahu-
     tells-foreign-press-calls-for-a-ceasefire-are-calls-for-israel-to-
     surrender/.
4   United Nations Office for the Coordination of Humanitarian
     Affairs, 'Hostilities in the Gaza Strip and Israel – Reported
     Impact – Day 145', United Nations Office for the Coordination of
     Humanitarian Affairs – occupied Palestinian territory, 29 February
     2024, http://www.ochaopt.org/content/hostilities-gaza-strip-and-
     israel-reported-impact-day-145.
5   Sederberg, 'Conciliation as Counter-Terrorist Strategy', p 298.

FURTHER READING

Robert J. Art and Louise Richardson, eds. *Democracy and Counterterrorism: Lessons from the Past* (United States Institute of Peace, 2007).

Michael J. Boyle, ed. *Non-Western Responses to Terrorism* (Manchester University Press, 2019).

David Cole and Jules Lobel, *Less Safe, Less Free* (The New Press, 2007).

Ronald Crelinsten, *Counterterrorism* (Polity Press, 2009).

Audrey Kurth Cronin, *How Terrorism Ends: Understanding the Decline and Demise of Terrorist Campaigns* (Princeton University Press, 2009).

Laura K. Donohue, *The Cost of Counterterrorism: Power, Politics, and Liberty* (Cambridge University Press, 2008).

Stuart Gottlieb, ed. *Debating Terrorism and Counterterrorism: Conflicting Perspectives on Causes, Contexts and Responses* (CQ Press, 2014).

Richard Jackson, *Writing the War on Terrorism: Language, Politics and Counter-Terrorism* (Manchester University Press, 2005).

Lee Jarvis and Michael Lister, eds. *Critical Perspectives on Counter-Terrorism* (Routledge, 2015).

David Keen, *Endless War? Hidden Functions of the 'War on Terror'* (Pluto Press, 2006).

Sondre Lindahl, *A Critical Theory of Counterterrorism: Ontology, Epistemology and Normativity* (Routledge, 2018).

Tom Parker, *Avoiding the Terrorist Trap: Why Respect for Human Rights is the Key to Defeating Terrorism* (World Scientific, 2019).

Senthil Ram and Ralph Summy, *Nonviolence: An Alternative for Defeating Global Terror(ism)* (Nova Publishers, 2008).

Paul Wilkinson, *Terrorism versus Democracy: The Liberal State Response* (Routledge, 2011).

Joseba Zulaika, *Terrorism: The Self-Fulfilling Prophecy* (University of Chicago Press, 2009).

INDEX

References to figures are in *italics*.